Gift
OF THE
Red Bird

Gift

OF THE

Red Bird

A Spiritual Encounter

PAULA D'ARCY

A Crossroad Book
The Crossroad Publishing Company
New York

Acknowledgment is gratefully given for permission to reprint from the following:

Page 7: "Sleeping in the Forest," from *Twelve Moons*, by Mary Oliver, copyright © 1978 by Mary Oliver. First appeared in *The Ohio Review*. By permission of Little, Brown and Company.

Page 58: "Wild Geese" by Mary Oliver from her collection *Dream Work* copyright © 1986 by Mary Oliver. Used by permission of Grove/Atlantic, Inc.

Page 71: Poem #816, from *The Complete Poems of Emily Dickinson*, reprinted by permission of Little, Brown and Company.

Page 90: "Little Gidding" in *Four Quartets,* copyright 1943 by T. S. Eliot and renewed 1971 by Esme Valerie Eliot, reprinted by permission of Harcourt Brace & Company.

Page 128: *The Prophet* by Kahlil Gibran, published by Alfred A. Knopf Incorporated, 1965, reprinted by permission of Random House, Inc.

1996

The Crossroad Publishing Company
370 Lexington Avenue, New York, NY 10017

Copyright © 1996 by Paula D'Arcy

Printed in the United States of America

Library of Congress Cataloging-in-Publication Data

D'Arcy, Paula, 1947-
 Gift of the red bird : a spiritual encounter / Paula D'Arcy.
  p. cm.
 ISBN 0-8245-1590-0
 1. D'Arcy, Paula, 1947- . 2. D'Arcy, Paula, 1947- .
 3. Spiritual biography – United States. 4. Vision quests.
 I. Title.
BL73.D37A3 1996
209'.2 – dc20
 [B]   96-19268
             CIP

For Eddie Sears,
the friend who taught me
about the power of prayer

I thought the earth
remembered me, she
took me back so tenderly, arranging
her dark skirts, her pockets
full of lichens and seeds. I slept
as never before, a stone
on the riverbed, nothing
between me and the white fire of the stars

—Mary Oliver, "Sleeping in the Forest"

Contents

Acknowledgments

I HAVE BEEN WRITING THIS BOOK for seven years, and even wrote and published a different book in the interim. Living with a writer can be difficult. Much time is spent churning things over in my mind and heart, and I can often be far away in thought. So with love I thank my daughter, Beth, for loving me anyway, and for putting up with the distance that sometimes happens. I especially thank her for being glad for me to go so often to the Texas hills, following my heart and God's call.

I am grateful beyond words to Laity Lodge in Leakey, Texas, for letting me live on their grounds in order to write, or simply to wander through the Frio Canyon, exploring my life and listening to the sounds of creation. That canyon home has given me more than I will ever be able to give back. It has been my teacher.

I thank John Godbey of Decatur, Alabama, for the gift of his talent as a photographer for the book cover photo. It is rare for me to find someone able to relax me in front of a camera. We were notably assisted by John Bentley, who stood knee deep in leaves for over an hour holding the glare screens. He made me laugh and always reminds me that friendships matter the most of all.

And I thank Lance Crawford (Strong Eagle), with whom I first led a Women's Gathering in 1991. The intensity of his faith has been a fire for my own. By inviting me to the desert in 1995, he gave me an opportunity to discover for myself that the desert is truly a mirror of the soul. It was there that I began to understand more fully the experiences contained in this book. His witness has helped me to find my way.

Introduction

I WRITE THESE WORDS sitting on a small square of red beach blanket, savoring a rare sixty-five-degree March afternoon on the Connecticut shore. The day is a gift. Beautiful white gulls fly out over the ocean, and my eyes slowly follow their graceful flight. Across the water, to the south, is the clear outline of Long Island Sound. I take a deep breath and listen with my eyes. This very spot is one of my cherished places of peace, and the finding of such a spot is not something I take for granted. It is, for me, a place of great stillness and importance.

Two thousand miles away, secreted in the Texas hills, is another such treasured location. In that oasis there is no sand, but rather palms, cactus, and gentle gray song birds. There I trade today's sandals for hiking shoes, and the sound of waves is replaced by the sweetest notes of the canyon wren. That land has also been my teacher. I have breathed in the wisdom of its canyon and have sat for hours watching midday light color the layers of rock, coaxing the tiniest petals to push for survival through dirt and stone. It was there I first learned to see what is essential. To see beauty. To see with my heart. To see that God, literally, is everywhere.

It is there that I first asked myself why we are able to master great technology, but do not yet understand our own hearts. Why, after centuries, are we still so far from understanding the nature of love? And why are we willing to make endless outer journeys, but are loath to make the significant one: the journey within. The inward journey may frighten us, yet it is this journey which holds the real treasure. There God's spirit waits to reveal mysteries and beauty beyond our imagination: the secrets of what is holy, and the encounters with truth that change everything. It is the journey that opens the eye of the heart.

This story is the telling of my own efforts to know God through listening within and by taking this journey. Following an inner call is not an easy task. It is contrary to all our conditioning, and especially to our culture's belief that logic is supreme. I had always admired those who were learned and wise and was convinced that those attributes of the mind would reveal the truth I sought. How unexpected to discover that the mind only supplied knowledge *about* God. Knowing God was different, and its sole requirement (in fact, the only way) was to be open like a child. That is the great step of faith: to become open and innocent in spirit. To see a familiar world for the first time. Nothing is more difficult.

As the story of a child must be, this story is simple and filled with surprises. The experiences which seemed least likely to further my awareness of God were precisely the ones which taught me the most. But new insights were often followed by years of inattention. I've learned this is not unusual. Awareness of God's presence seems to weave in and out of the fabric of our years, often followed by prolonged periods of apparent heavenly silence. But fruitfulness can never be measured by activity. Whether or not I was aware of it, I was always "on my way."

I was also surprised at how often I heard God's voice with the greatest clarity through encounters with traditions that were not my own. I've come to understand that the "familiar" can be a great barrier to new revelations. My original expectations about the manner of God's presence were so set. Bit by bit those expectations had to be dismantled so I would be able to see what was, rather than what I expected or had even been taught. It was surrendering to God, rather than to my cherished image of God. The difference is the key.

I fill these pages with deep humility. My story, as history, is unimportant to anyone but me. But all of our stories, as spiritual journeys, matter. We affect one another. We are all reflections of a great Mystery.

As I write these words a seagull calls out boldly above my head, and the wind blows sand into my thermos of tea. I consider the wonder of a bird's flight, or even the journey of the wind. I envy them. They know their way already, and I am just beginning.

> *Always be in a state of expectancy,*
> *and see that you leave room*
> *For God to come in as He likes.*
>
> —Oswald Chambers

One

THE GOD OF MY CHILDHOOD was masculine. He was stern, judgmental, remote, and all-controlling. If I was good enough, he approved of me. So I tried to be very, very good and said rote prayers with all my heart. I considered "sinful" half of my human thoughts and most of my moments of expression. Sacrifice atoned for my sins. Sacrifice, and striving toward perfection. I also believed that priests, nuns, ministers, rabbis, and religious masters reached God. Those ordained or chosen, not ordinary people. Otherwise, why did we consider them the authorities, and why were we always looking to them and not to our own hearts?

I understood revelation as something that had begun and ended two thousand years ago. We *learned* about it, past tense. There were two worlds, one secular and one spiritual. Good people learned to control their secular impulses. The spiritual world, though dry and uninteresting, was the goal. It was the world that was good.

I had many questions about God when I was young. But I could not find adults with satisfying answers or with a theology expansive enough to contain any of my questions alongside their truths. So my understanding of God was confined to the head of a pin, and the little, narrow, remote God who could fit there held very little attraction. All through college I continued to worship this small idol, equating faith with being on my knees and equating spiritual journey with restriction, deprivation, and "shoulds." Unconsciously, religion and guilt became linked in my psyche.

Who could love a faith so burdensome? So at age twenty-two, without much forethought, I simply walked away from the whole dreary package. Enough perfection. Enough sacrifice. Enough being "good." If the message was that miserable, I could find other avenues to express my joy. It was an abrupt choice. It happened in a moment. I turned my back on everything I had learned before and felt a taste of what I called freedom. I stopped going to church and stopped having "religious" thoughts. I simply began to fully experience my life.

I read once that the soul is not discovered in the heavens, but on earth. Some inner instinct of mine must have known that. At the time I was only aware of a desire to discover and be who I was. In theological terms, I suppose I was finally risking incarnation. *My* incarnation. Ironically, at this very moment when I believed myself to be walking away from God, I was closest to encountering him for myself. I was only walking away from someone else's conclusions about God and from someone else's roadway. What beckoned me was the roadway which was my own and the God who would not be an idea, but a Presence I was invited to encounter. Every sincere seeker wrestles with this moment and the Mystery beyond it.

July 1972, Age 24

It's just six months prior to my wedding, and I'm packing my lemon yellow VW convertible (bicycles strapped to the back) and am heading west from New England with my sister, Beverly, to visit our sister, Barby, and her husband, Jim, in their Bozeman, Montana, home. I feel young and in full charge of my destiny.

Week One

We travel as interest and stamina lead us, some days accomplishing five hundred miles, other days only twelve. I feel as if I'm soaking up the towns along our route, and I love listening to the stories of the different people we encounter. Today we found a drugstore with a 1940's soda fountain. We bought old-fashioned cherry cokes made with squirts from the original seltzer pump.

I do a lot of thinking as we drive. I think about my upcoming marriage and the possible loss of independence it could mean. I wonder about freedom, imagining it to be a sustained state of "being able to do exactly as I please." I like the freedom I'm experiencing right now, navigating our way through cities and towns. After the crowded East, the endless highways of the West are thrilling. The miles offer astonishing mountain scenery and desolate, flat lowlands.

Week Two

Today we reached Montana, and the famous sky... which *is* richly and memorably blue! The sheer space and the smell of clean air make everything seem freshly created. Barby and Jim have now joined us for further adventures. First we'll head toward Jackson Hole, Wyoming, and Yellowstone Park. Then Jim wants us to visit an Arapaho Indian reservation in Wind River, Wyoming, where one of his college students has invited us to be present for the Sun Dance, a sacred Indian ceremony. I suppose this will be a pleasant aside. My trip has already been filled with high moments and many attractions.

Week Three

Today we arrived at Wind River Reservation. The reservation is dust swept and hotter than I've ever been or wanted to be. The relentless sun of Wyoming, I think to myself. My eye and senses have grown accustomed to Glacier Park and lush Montana. Now this: miles and miles of brown clay mixed with dirt, scant vegetation, and a poverty of shade. We meet Jim's student, Dennis Sun Rhodes. He greets us warmly and talks about the Sun Dance, which will begin the next day. He says that the ceremony symbolizes his people's close relationship with the supernatural. For four days the dancers will fast and dance, their actions a prayer and offering to God, whom they call the Great Spirit. I am struck by how closely these people live to nature. Even the time of the Sun Dance is related to the cycle of the moon. It is strange to me.

I watch the final preparations of the Sun Dance Lodge. Every item placed inside the lodge (drums, feathers, tufts of sage) is brought in and laid down so carefully. I ask and am told that everything they use is a symbol relating to nature, and to human nature. That remark catches me. Dennis speaks about human beings as interconnected to every living thing. His people understand nature as filled with meaning, created by the same Spirit whose breath fills all living things. Observe and listen to nature, they believe, and the Great Spirit will teach you about your own nature and the truths for which the heart is hungry.

And suddenly I am standing apart, still watching, but thinking about my life. I think of the boxes of Corning Ware, silver, and crystal already amassed for my upcoming wedding. I think of the hours I've already spent debating furniture styles and choosing fabric for bridesmaids' dresses. I live, supposedly, in the hub of a very enlightened twentieth century. I have attended churches and cathedrals with magnificent stained glass and massive steeples whose painting and repair require committees and by-laws. I have access to Bible translations and interpretations, histories of the church and libraries of theological criticism. And yet, baking in the sun on this forsaken stretch of dirt on the Western Plains, I am oddly wondering if all my knowledge has possibly brought me precious little truth.

I wander back to a small pavilion and buy some beaded earrings, fingering the array of blankets and baskets displayed there. I note the bright colors and remember once reading that to Native people seeing is sacred. Something about seeing the real world through the eye of the heart. The thought makes me uncomfortable. I know I take seeing for granted.

I keep walking around restlessly. I watch the Sun Dance preparations for a while, then I pace. I'm certainly not uninterested. I just feel overwhelmed, and I don't know why. I came here as a tourist, to take a polite look at another culture's ceremony. But instead, I am feeling confused by mysterious stirrings in my heart. I can't help but wonder, if Eden had not been destroyed, would this consciousness of theirs be everyone's? Could it be mine? I shut out all the conversations around me and consider the idea that nothing is separate, and that the earth, stars, trees, animals...everything...might be a sacred expression of God. Is everything holy?

A cottonwood tree is positioned at the center of the lodge. I learn that when the upper limb of a cottonwood is cut crosswise, the grain reveals a perfect, five-pointed star. The star is understood as a sign of the Great Spirit's presence and the tree's holy nature. Even the breeze blowing through the cottonwood leaves is understood to be its prayer.

Prayer. I think in feeble contrast of *my* experience

of thees and thous... of sanctuaries and proper meeting houses... of booklets, printed by the hundreds of thousands, entitled "How to Pray." I think of my many prayers of petition, prayers for comfort, prayers to be protected from harm. But prayers always very unconcerned with any meaning of life which didn't spill onto my own doorstep. I wonder, watching, if I really understand what it means to pray, and if I would lose my inner restlessness if I did.

I look for a while longer at the cottonwood tree, thinking about it nestling its five-pointed star. I think of the housing developments we passed on our way to the reservation. I consider all the trees that were felled without a thought to supply that lumber. The forests ruined. Stars chopped down. Choked. Who would ever notice, in my busy life, that a star is secreted in a cottonwood tree? It makes me wonder, are there equally hidden depths inside of me?

Two more days have passed and I am transfixed, watching the dance. My sister comments, "What's wrong with you? Are you mesmerized?" They go off to do other things, but I can't leave. I am watching people dance their prayer... they are praying with their whole being. My eyes are captivated and also my ears.

The drumming is incessant, and the beat has gotten inside of me. It's like hearing my own heartbeat for the first time.

Today the dancing is over, and Dennis and his family invite me into their tepee to participate in a closing ritual. It feels quiet and reverent inside as I sit cross-legged on the ground, hushed. A bowl of sweet grass and water is passed, and as I raise it, in turn, to my own lips, I feel tears spilling from my eyes. I cry because I am aware that they know something that all my education has not taught me. For a moment, sitting in the dimmed light of this circle, my heart opens and I experience God through someone else's eyes. I hear God in a way I never have before. I am grasping something...a small piece of a great wonder. The moment feels strangely holy, although nothing in my background has prepared me to recognize holiness from such a source. For a moment I hold their openness in my own arms. I am moved, as if the Great Spirit has called my own name.

Is that possible? Could I trust it? I wonder who ever convinced me that God will only reveal himself to me in certain ways? I will leave this reservation with many questions. Many of these Indians live in great poverty.

But do those of us with greater wealth really have more? I would give anything for their connectedness with life. Do the possessions I continue to accumulate make me feel more connected, or less? What does it really mean to see with the eye of the heart?

Following this experience I returned to my life and my carefully laid out plans. I packed away my summer's journal to make space for the wedding finery. Once in a while, and then less and less often, I thought of the days at Wind River and the questions they had raised. I was busy and my days full. I was too cluttered to remember that secreted in my depths, there might be a star.

Two

*I*N JANUARY 1973 I was married to Roy D'Arcy. Ten months later we celebrated the birth of our daughter, Sarah. My life had never seemed so rich, fairly bursting with promise. Sarah filled every waking (and several nonwaking) hours, but the task of mothering was one I'd chosen and relished. When Roy wasn't at home spending time with Sarah and/or me, he was teaching English classes at a nearby community college or busy digging up our backyard in order to create a vegetable garden productive enough to feed the Western hemisphere. The garden was his place of contemplation and joy.

Our budget was limited and our life simple. But even so, friends made our lives full, and Roy's unquenchable thirst for books and knowledge occupied many hours. When nights were long or our hearts troubled, he read poetry out loud. We often fell asleep with the words of great masters ringing in our rooms and comforting our spirits. In June 1975 we learned that I was again pregnant. I felt proudly on the brink of every dream. In August of that year we traveled from our Connecticut home to Massachusetts to share the excitement in person with my parents. I was looking ahead with assurance, never guessing that this trip could end with senseless tragedy.

But as we returned home to Connecticut on August 18, our car was struck by a drunken motorist who careened across a divided interstate highway where the required metal safety barrier had been "overlooked" and never installed. The driver's speed was ninety-seven miles per hour. Sarah died of head injuries on August 20, and Roy died three days later from a ruptured spleen. I was twenty-seven years old, three months pregnant, miraculously alive, and shattered beyond any sense. I wished I too had died, and couldn't imagine ever feeling differently. The long journey of grief would consume the agonizing years which followed. I gave birth to my second daughter, Beth, on March 20, 1976. For her sake I fought my way back to sanity, filled with questions, fears, and disillusionment about life. The greatest question was: How could a loving God let this happen?

August 1975, Age 27

I blink my eyes and all I love is gone...becomes a dream. No goodbyes. No considerations. My life will never be the same. I inhale and I am a mother and wife; I exhale and there is utter darkness and I am a grieving widow with no child to hold. It feels as if someone has hurled a hot brick against my chest and my hands cannot take it off. Nothing can take it off. Life has become hideous and I am powerless. Totally powerless. I cannot change this, and I desperately want someone to make it go away. All I loved is gone.

I lie in my hospital room and moan. A tidal wave has swept over me and I am trying to hold it back with my bare hand. I cry from so deep inside of me...deeper than I've ever known. I cry because my hand is so small and the wave so powerful. I am not strong enough. I am at the bottom of a black pit, and I don't care.

October 1975

People tell me I am brave. Only I know that I hang onto sanity by a thread. My every step is along the edge of a precipice. Any false moves now and I will never recover. My need to know what is true is crucial. God is real, or he isn't. There is hope, or life is a cruel joke. There is hope, or life is meaningless. My life depends on these answers. You can't endure the pain I am feeling for ultimate meaninglessness. You couldn't be convinced to do it. I will only live if there is truth and glory and blinding light. I have to know.

November 1975

There is one advantage to having your life cut through to the bone. It swiftly eliminates all the distractions and all the illusions. The clarity of my sight is fierce. I see what matters and what does not. And if I am going to find God, he will encounter no resistance. No games. No asking for signs. Just come. I am split open. God will come all the way in, if he is out there at all.

December 1975

In this abyss I am learning what it means to really pray. To pray as if your very life depended upon it. Mine does. I guess my life has always depended upon something outside of myself. But in this abyss, I know it. I pray as if finding the truth about life is the difference between sanity and senselessness. For me, it is. My anger is spent now, my eyes and throat changed by tears. I have kicked and screamed at my enormous sense of betrayal by everything I have believed in. Marriage. Family. Love. Plans. Goodness. Being a good person doesn't mean life won't wound you. None of the protections I believed in were real. And now I am left either resenting my life because I didn't get the things I wanted, or learning to love life on its own terms. Really, learning to accept God on his own terms. It is very, very quiet inside of me. My first honest prayer is a whisper. "God, if you are really out there, help me. Let me find you."

January 1976

I scream, *Why?* For months I have screamed, *Why?* Why did this happen to me? Wasn't I good enough? Am I being punished? Could you have controlled this, God, but didn't? *Why?* Do you hate me? I only stop asking why when I sleep.

Then I feel a Presence next to me, down here in the abyss. I don't know how I know that. I just know. Something is different. I am not alone. It's as if someone is saying to me, LOOK. USE YOUR EYES. SEE. And so out of my depths I begin to look into people's eyes for the first time in my life, and I am startled by what I see. So many people are unhappy. Many are bitter. Most people look without seeing. That has been me. I am looking in a mirror. But some eyes are different. They are filled with a certain light, and it draws me like a laser. I want it. Sliced open, unable to be fooled, I see that the light is good. How did they get it? I need to know.

I begin to see something else. The people with the bitter, unseeing eyes avoid my pain. They are uncomfortable with it...with me. They want me to be myself again and to stop reminding them that life is treacherous. But the people with the light-filled eyes are not frightened by my grief. Some admit that they don't begin to understand it. But none of them can be dissuaded from their belief that God is with me in it. They say he has never left me. Would not. In fact, he is in the abyss with me, waiting. And he will stay with me, as long as it takes. Love and unconditional acceptance surround my pit. They are real. There is something deeper than the abyss.

I eat those words like my first meal after a long fast. They would be merely words, except for the light. I think about it. A God who stays with me. Not someone far away. Not someone only the clergy can reach. Not someone confined to Bibles and prayerbooks and sanctuaries. A God so personal and loving that he is in this pit with me. A God who is close and real. Yet he asks so much. He asks me to look at wrecked cars and stolen lives...to stare straight ahead at only darkness and believe in light. He asks me to change and to see differently. But maybe not so difficult to do in my circumstances. I have tried everything else. Nothing else I know can pierce the darkness and turn it back. Not perfection. Or hard work. Not control. Not even the best values. If any of these things had the power to endure,

I would have seen it. I would know. But they were all moveable. So here I am in the dark, in the face of being refused the people and the life I wanted the most. My future is utterly unknown. There is nothing to guide me but a light. There is nothing to assure me but faith. And yet, I am about to take the first step. I am suspending all I have been taught in order to follow my own path. Perhaps I will reach some of the same conclusions with which I was raised. But this will be different. They will no longer be premises. I will own them. They are right to call it a leap. It is.

February 1976

I slowly begin to understand that it is up to me to choose how I will respond to this pain. I can let it eat me, and grow my own bitter eyes. Or I can let go of my assumptions about how life should be, and search for the beauty in what life is. It's like bread loaves from crumbs. The pieces of my life transformed into something beautiful. Tears into joy. Mourning into dancing. It is a choice. I can barely believe that God is with me in this pit for as long as it takes. Why? Why me? Days ago I was demanding to know *Why me*, why am I so cursed? Now I am asking, Why am I so blessed? I also have this growing conviction that when God first came to me in response to my prayer he dimmed himself. I know he is blinding white light. But I could never have withstood the brightness. Somehow that gesture moves me more than a thousand miracles.

March 1976

My body readies itself to give birth. I shudder with fear that this child too may die. I have never been more aware that life is fragile. The deepest desire of my heart is to have a healthy, natural birth ... and, hopefully, another little girl to love. After so much death, every cell in my body wants to experience life. I have asked God to promise me at least that.

The baby is ready, I am ready, but my body won't go into labor. My fear is too great, I'm sure. My doctor sends me to the hospital for a caesarean, but because of my pleading he induces my labor first to give me a last chance at a normal delivery. With full force of my will I command my body into labor. But it remains frozen. I am prepped for surgery and take myself off to a corner of the labor room, sit in a green wing chair, and close my eyes. "God," I say. Just that. "God." I feel anger rising up. The words, "God, what do you want?" finally come out. "What do you want from me? You have my husband. You have my daughter. I'm fighting so hard to accept my life as it is. To trust you. I haven't asked for anything else except this natural birth. What more do you want from me?"

There is nothing but my tears for several moments. Then I hear a voice within me. The voice is distinct. Clear. Loving. It says, PAULA, I WANT YOU TO WANT ME MORE THAN YOU WANT ANYTHING.

Two or three nurses are moving around me. The anesthesiologist is present, waiting. But my inner reality is suddenly more deafening than the everyday world of which I am a part. LOOK AT YOURSELF, I hear God gently saying. REALLY SEE YOURSELF. SEE HOW YOU HOLD ONTO THINGS. WHATEVER COMES FIRST...WHATEVER YOU WANT THE MOST...WHATEVER YOU HAVE TO HAVE, BECOMES YOUR GOD. PUT ME FIRST. THAT WILL CHANGE EVERYTHING.

Without trying I am suddenly seeing my life through a different set of eyes. I see clearly that my daughter, Sarah, has been my god. Yes, I loved her, as a mother should. But I also clung to her. I thought I owned her. I made her my purpose for living. She was not a soul with whose care I had been entrusted. She was someone I believed to be mine. I see her and all my other false gods. I hear God's words and I see the difference between what he is saying and what I have done. It is hushed and quiet. I am weary beyond description. I asked for answers and I am receiving them. I suspect that I am being taught universal, spiritual law. I am at the end of me, I know that. With my eyes still shut, I finally relinquish the need to be right and to have my own way. I stop trying to be god. If I weren't so top-heavy I'd be on my knees. Inside, I am on my knees. I have surrendered. I give God me, including the way I wanted things to be and the answers I needed to have. I not only accept God's plan for my life, I seek it. "Go ahead," I say. "You lead and I'll follow. This operation isn't what I had in mind, but I'll make it through. Just don't leave me." It is so still.

Then, unexpectedly, I am filled with freedom. *Filled* with freedom. I do not feel a little bit free. I feel outrageously, tremendously free. Walking-on-air free. Ten-inches-off-the-ground free. I am a pathetic single woman, stripped of everything and about to bear a child I can scarcely support. And yet none of it matters. There is nothing left that I desire more than God. I own nothing, but more importantly, nothing owns me. I am no longer resisting.

Then just as swiftly as my joy has come, it is eclipsed by tremendous pain. Pain as if my very bones are moving. I laugh to myself and ask the nurses to get the doctor. I am ready to give birth and I know it. I won't need their knife. I am free and so is my body. I am ready. The nurses roll their eyes. They think I have gone over the edge. The doctor is already scrubbed for surgery and doesn't want to come. For my own safety he is anxious to proceed. The x-rays and the statistics are all contrary to my proclaimed readiness. But he checks me anyway, probably to appease me. Then they are all quiet. When they move again it is to take me to the delivery room. And before any of us can grasp it we are looking at my daughter Beth. Born naturally. Born in joy.

I hold Beth in my arms to nurse her. She is amazing, but the real birth today was my own. As I look at her I see that she is a gift. She is mine to hold, but not to possess. It makes all the difference. You treat a gift differently than you do a possession. And God loved me enough to show me how to relinquish her before I would ever embrace her. If I hadn't learned this, given my grief, I fear I would have smothered us both. I weep because God was willing to stick it out with me through all my anger and all my despair, wanting me to be healed more deeply than I could have believed possible. I have received so much more than I asked for.

August 1976

This year has been harder than any days I have lived. Yet in a strange way I also call this period my glory days. Days of stark pain and bright light. They convince me that the wells for pain and joy are not separate. I have never hurt so badly, nor seen such brilliance. Simultaneously. I have been to the bottom of the pit, and Love was deeper still. The power of Love is greater than the power of pain. It is a fact. The knowing is in me. I have seen through so much illusion, even though I suffered greatly to gain the sight. Now I know that the real powers are of the Spirit.

Three

ETTING MY LIFE BACK IN ORDER after tragedy ripped it apart became the centerpiece of all my efforts for the following seven years. Some of the days and events were inspiring and encouraging, but many of them required plain hard work and the development of my growing faith. In 1979 the journal of my losses and grief process were published as my first book, *Song for Sarah*. With that publication came an overwhelming number of invitations to speak, lead retreats or workshops, and be interviewed.

I stepped into the public circle innocently, with sincere, hard-won beliefs. My faith, born in the depths of adversity, was fresh and true. But it was not accompanied by any awareness of the pitfalls I might encounter. I knew little about taking care of myself, and even less about taking care of the soul-space within me where I'd heard God. Soon I was overcome by the demands on my hours. The requests to "tell my story" in order to help and encourage others were seemingly endless. I found myself searching for more and more hours to give, and wearing thin doing "good" deeds. Since the hours requested of me could not materialize from the ether, I began to rob my interior time bit by bit in order to have enough of me to go around. This happened slowly and unsuspectingly, every decision seeming to make perfect sense. I did not betray myself in one grandstand moment. I repeated it in small, polite ones until my habit of doing so determined my life. Repeatedly I spent less and less time *with* God, but in order to do more things *for* him.

I was chipping away at myself, but gently. I couldn't hear it happening. Eventually I was aware of being physically tired, but I didn't remember that my body is deeply connected to my mind and my soul. I raced on with confidence, while everything began to erode.

Fall 1982, Age 34

I feel so tired tonight, so defeated. I sit down at my desk to write and can't even find a clear space. I'm desperately afraid that this desk is a perfect picture of me: an array of clutter and important things left unopened. Suddenly my life seems to be going a hundred miles an hour. I find myself dashing out for grocery items fifteen minutes before a meal. The right article of clothing is never ironed when I need it. Every Friday morning I sprint to the curb in my nightgown, racing to put out the trash bags before the truck screeches to a halt at my driveway.

What is wrong? Inside of me, mimicking the outer disharmony, grows a restlessness I can't quite name. A longing to be free of everything, maybe. To be out from under the pressure of trying to be so many things that I can't remember what it means to just be myself. Some sane part of me reasons that you can't know *anyone* without spending time with that person. So doesn't that go for me, too? How can I know myself if I am constantly busy and never alone?

Last night I read Beth *The Velveteen Rabbit.* It is hard for me to read it without tears. I think it's painful because it tugs at such a deep yearning. I want to be real. What would it feel like not to be caught up in any more doing or performing? Not to measure most of my decisions against the expectations of others, but against my honest feelings? Today I found an old yellowed piece of paper inside a book. Apparently I wrote these words years ago:

> Why do adults hide? We are so serious, so intent on measuring and building. We are caught up exploring every inch of the space we inhabit. We probe molecules for their secrets. We hurl ourselves into the reaches of space. We design passageways over rivers and measure the distance to the stars. We even plumb the ocean depths. We'd do anything not to journey inside.

In *The Velveteen Rabbit*, the bunny begins to see the tender, concealed part of himself, the heart of him, and understands that to accept and feel his honest emotions is an excellent beginning if one chooses to be real. Is the core of that rabbit really any different than the core of me? I, too, feel like a collection of honest emotions: fears, feelings, insecurities, longings. It's the truth about myself, but I hardly ever bring it to the light. I keep growing chronologically but hide this real self further and further away.

Have I traded in the truth of myself for the polish of my public image? The thought is hard to swallow, as hard as the real, physical lump I've felt in my throat for days. I know I should have it checked, and I will, when there is time.

Nighttime. I am again exhausted. My throat hurts, my head aches, and I feel as if I would weep if someone offered to serve my dinner or wash my floor. I feel the full weight of being a single parent. I fill the twenty-four hours given to me, and I need six more. I push myself every waking minute. I am not living, I am trudging through. I get things done from sheer determination, but I hardly ever enjoy anything anymore.

Today I physically collapsed. I suppose there is always a breaking point, and I found mine. I have just returned from an eight-day speaking tour in Canada, and I simply could not go on. I gladly got driven to the doctor to have this throat lump — which has grown into an ugly, white outcropping — looked at. I just want them to cut it out.

The doctor is annoyingly cautious. He feels my

glands, checks my fever, takes blood. I just want him to cut this thing out so I can go on my way. I don't have the strength to wait for blood tests. I sleep soundly in the waiting room and am awakened with his words that his unlikely suspicion is confirmed. I have a throat abscess and a raging case of mononucleosis. I laugh out loud. I think it's funny. Hooray! Inwardly there is a secret relief. I can lie in bed for a week without guilt, catch up on a few good books, and be legitimately excused from my life. A seven-day respite is a heaven-sent gift. With a detailed plan for my unstructured recuperation, I *finally* lay down to rest.

Seven days have passed and I haven't yet had the strength to even hold a newspaper or magazine, let alone read one. The week I allowed myself to get well is over, and I am hardly ready for action. This morning I faced my first sinking realization that this disease is in control, not me.

Weeks have now passed and I am still too weak to get out of bed. At night I crawl on my hands and knees to get to the adjoining bathroom. The energy required for that effort seems so great. I barely have the strength to breathe. With every breath I feel as if clamps have been tightened around my chest. The clamps are definitely winning. Worse than the persisting fevers, nausea, and aching throat is this feeling that I can't really breathe.

How do I fight back against this intruder into my body's system? I lie awake for hours in the middle of the night and sob. My instincts tell me that when attacked, you fight back. But fighting back is not working. Fighting back requires the strength I lack. Everyone says, "Give in. Rest." But the truth is, I don't know how.

I sink back into my pillows and grow more and more depressed. Tears come frequently, each tide washing away more of my scant hope. I remember who I used to be, but I don't know how to get that vibrant person back. I despair that I ever will. Fighting back from the accident already took my allotted reserves. I can't fight back a second time.

Winter 1982–83

Beth has been complaining that she doesn't feel well. Headaches. Nausea. She has dark circles under her eyes. She deserves a mother, and the one she has barely has the strength to heat a casserole which someone else has prepared. Then I collapse on the couch, trying to regain my breath. We never go anywhere or do anything. Beth plays with dolls at my bedside or leans up against the couch where I lie, toys strewn at her feet. My tears heave out of me in big silent cries. What kind of life is this for a seven-year-old girl who started suffering even before she was born? I feel as if I am failing at everything I try to do. Now I can do nothing, and my uselessness smothers me. I *was* at least a writer and a speaker. I touched lives. Now I am nobody.

Beth continues to look pale, and is sent home from school every six or seven days. I keep telling the doctor I'm afraid she has mono. But he doesn't believe it will happen. He reassures me. Still, after weeks of her distress I finally convince him to do the blood test. It never felt worse to be right.

We stretch out on opposite couches and allow neighbors and friends to bring us hot foods rich in iron and protein. We watch "People's Court" until I feel qualified to pass the bar exam, and day by day Beth brightens and regains her strength. After a short period of home tutoring she is back in her classroom, filled with energy, color in her cheeks. The day she leaves I cry my heart out. I cry because I miss her cheery presence, but mostly I cry because she has achieved what I cannot. She has gotten well.

I lie flat on my back again today, staring at the cracks in the wall. I hear the outside door open, noting distantly the signal I've established with friends to let me know when someone is bringing in food or perhaps stopping by for a brief visit. It's difficult to imagine who would want to visit me. I am pathetic. I look wretched, I have no cheer, no news, no interest, and no consolation. That I have a steady stream of visitors, people who haven't given up on me, amazes me. One friend pulls a chair next to my bedside today and listens without comment to my stream of complaints, which is my excuse for a greeting. I know how I sound, but I can't seem to do better. Then it's quiet for a long while. He seems to hesitate, probably measuring the potential wrath of my reaction against the value of his words. Finally he looks me in the eye and says, slowly and carefully, "Paula, did you figure it out yet?" I am in no mood for games and guesses. I mutter, "Did I figure *What* out yet?"

He is not daunted by me. "Did you figure out what the war is all about inside of you? What's wrong in your soul?"

I hope my returning glare is strong. I want to cry, but don't want to give him the satisfaction. Eventually he shrugs his shoulders and leaves.

The problem with his words is that they fill the room and leave me no hiding place. All night long they keep me awake. What is wrong in my *soul?* I thought what is wrong is wrong in my body. My symptoms are all physical. But even so, could the roots of my unrest be spiritual?

I think of the power of naming. I remember a graduate school professor who insisted you could never solve a problem you could not accurately name. Am I really out of harmony with God? Aren't I run down and exhausted from doing *his* work? Isn't that what the spiritual path is all about? And if not, then what *is* it all about? I stare out the window, watching the snow fall. I realize that I missed fall this year. Missed a season. Never got outside. Never noticed the leaves. Then it occurs to me that maybe this isn't the first time I've missed a season. I have been oblivious to so many days. But this is the first time I've known it.

I consider the fact that my aches and pains may be glaring witnesses to a dangerous state in my being. I turn on my side and rearrange my pillows so I can really watch the snow. The tears that fall now are the first gentle ones. The snow is beautiful and I *see* it. I *see* it. God feels closer than he has in months. I shut my eyes for a few moments and hug the bed covers around my chin. I need to learn how to live. It is suddenly very clear.

It is a new morning and I take it in. I may have overcome tremendous odds in my life. I may have scaled all the mountains and gotten tremendous admiration for having done so. I do know how to survive. I did it. But I am beginning to see that that journey was only the one to get my attention. It was the backdrop. If I were in a theater, that journey was the set design, the scenery. But now the *real* landscape is in front of me. The interior landscape. The one about which I know very little.

I am thoughtful for twenty-four hours. Beth says I "look funny." I probably look half-way peaceful and she is unaccustomed to that face, it's been so long. The afternoon sun edges my bedroom window and I see it. I close my eyes to pray. My constant, continual, nagging prayer has been to be physically well. Today, the prayer changes. I pray, in fact, that I will *not* get well. Not until I can thoroughly reevaluate the quality of my life. I need to learn what life is about. What *my* life is about.

I repeat the prayer over and over. I am no longer desperate to be healthy in body, but in spirit. I want to find truth. What a dangerous prayer, if I mean it.

Now I begin to review the past four or five years of my life. The truth wounds my pride. I see that since my whole career of writing and public speaking began, there was never a moment when I consciously decided, This is the path I should follow. Nor did I ever ask God, Is this the way you want me to go? I made a lot of assumptions.

All the events, invitations, and coincidences catapulted me onto certain roads, and I went along with them. It was Christian ministry, so of course it was good. I never asked the question, but is it right for *me?* Is it right *at this time?* Right *at this pace?* It never occurred to me that simply because a deed or mission was good in nature, and because it was put before me, it didn't necessarily mean that I was the one to fulfill it, even if I did have the talents to do so. There is nothing inherently sacred about an act of service. It can bless you or lead you astray. My arms had been filled with acts of service and God was now saying to me, You have no room for me.

The truth hurts. I have had no time in my life for

God. Me, who went through so much to even be willing to look in his direction. I only make time to do things *for* him. I do not create time to be *with* him. My life has had no stillness and no space. My life has no silence.

I am starting to see what I do. I accept the goals and directions which seem to spill into my lap, and then I begin to fashion them. I work hard to do things well. I work hard to make the path in front of me a useful one. I work hard at everything and I have no time for God.

Lying here in my bed, without distractions, I see how prone I am to run headlong into people's needs. But by living in this way, I give away pieces of my life. Important pieces. Pieces of my energy, my time, my strength. On the basis of assumptions (This *must* be right) as opposed to intentions (I *choose* to go this way), I have given over ownership of me. Willingness to help is healthy, but a need to help is not.

I consider the fact that God might have created me with special purpose. Maybe I need to think about what I am here on earth to do. But to find that I need to be able to recognize my own preferences and my own needs. That's the hard part. I am so programed to respond to others, I don't know me at all. It feels wrong to think that my own needs, wants, and desires are important. It feels selfish. At least, that's what my programing says. What an irony if in fact they are very important to know. What if a way I discover God is through really being me?

I have to laugh. I have taken better care of some of my cars than I have of me. I wouldn't set fire to my home, but I have been willing to set fire to myself. No wonder I am ill. It's surprising only that I am not even sicker.

What words have lured me so completely away from myself? The possibilities float in front of me. "You're so special, and we're counting on you to do this." "No one else can do it." "You've *got* to be there." "If you can't do it, it won't get done." And against the clamor of these choruses was God's small voice asking, "Can't you spend just one hour with me?" I am ashamed of my answer. My "no." The habit of "doing" rather than "being" is hard-fast inside of me.

I've been in bed for eight months and I've cried many tears. I've wept with illness, frustration, and anger. Now I weep with sight. Finally, I cry tears that will heal.

Spring 1983

I start taking portions of my bedridden day and give them to God. I am unpracticed at this. It isn't easy. I read a little scripture and think about the words. I look out the window, oddly comforted by the trees. I talk to God in my head, telling him what I'm thinking. I am honest, for once in my life. I realize that I even had a way of coming before God and trying to do it perfectly. Wanting to seem holy, I guess. I give all of that up. I just tell God how I really feel. I say that I hurt. I say that building back my life has been too hard. I let the real tears come out. No more bravery. Just a struggling human being. I tell God that I do not want answers, miracles, or moving mountains. I only want a friend. I want peace inside.

It feels so good to be real. To be both strong and weak. A lot of weight begins to lift. I will succeed and I will also fail. I don't have to just succeed in order to be valued. Maybe I will even be likeable as a whole person, one with roundedness and failings. At least, *I'm* starting to like myself this way, and God seems to accept me. Some small peace roots itself inside of me and begins to grow.

I find a poem called "Wild Geese." The first three lines make me laugh at myself. They are the expression of all that God is teaching me:

> *You do not have to be good.*
> *You do not have to walk on your knees*
> *for a hundred miles through the desert, repenting.*

I laugh because it's silly, and I cry because it's true. That's me. Walking on my knees for a hundred miles . . . I'll do it. I'll get it right. Now God is suggesting a treasonous thought: Just sit still and love my earth. Find its beauty. Go sit there with me.

Bit by bit I am feeling better. I don't want to tell anyone though, and I wonder why. I think part of me doesn't want to rush all I am learning until I learn it well. I still fear being swallowed up again. Right now I wake up anxious for the present day. My interior landscape is less threatening now that I've spent some time there. I don't want to stop learning about this land. I also don't want to jinx the first signs of physical recovery by announcing them too soon. It has been a long year. Can I *really* be well again?

"Thank you for another day," I whisper each morning. The sheets on my bed feel good. The light coming through the window is a gift. How do I want to live out this day? I look at the African violet on my windowsill. If I don't water it, it will die. I see that my spirit is no different. I am beginning to listen a lot. The silence is my water.

I see that in the last few years I lost myself in the roles I was playing. Mother. Author. Speaker. Friend. Counselor. Rather than these roles being channels for God to use in certain seasons of my life, they *became* my life. They became my security and my identity. They were how I saw myself, and who I thought I was. When I was stripped of them, I felt like nothing.

Instead of being a facet of me, these roles became my worth. As they moved, changed, disappeared, I did, too. Now I am working hard to find and love the person *behind* the roles. The real me. The child of God. When I know her my roles can return to being roles, expendable and fleeting. I filled some of these roles so that others would approve of me. Now I am learning to approve of myself. It leaves room for my god to be God, and not the voices and approval of others. The power of this insight is worth all the months in bed.

I think about my early prayers for strength, health,

and peace of mind. I wanted it to fall from the bedroom ceiling. I didn't want to work for it. I wanted an instant cure. I prayed for my body to be well as I was simultaneously misusing it. I begged to find peace while I pressed my nervous system to the bone. I am pretty funny.

Today I am making a list: "Who has my life belonged to?"

> The telephone
> My child
> Appointments
> My career
> My church
> My friends
> The television
> My need for approval
> My guilt

Writing it down feels like casting my own lots. Written down, in black and white, many of my owners seem insane. Why have I given anyone or anything permission to run my life? How did I wind up responsible to so many things, but not myself? It has taken a lot to get me to think these thoughts. And even if I'd written this list several months ago and had listed God, it would have been a lie. I talked about him a lot, but hardly knew him at all. It was more comfortable to have ideas and theories about him, than to have a real ongoing encounter.

This evening I sit on my deck, enjoying the moon. I look again at my list. It would be easy to criticize myself, but that won't solve anything. Only waking up will change things. I take a sharp black marker and remake the inventory. I write God at the top, and me second. My child is third. I scratch out the television. The noise it creates is half of the reason I am seldom quiet. It pretends to fill an emptiness. But it only fills space. The emptiness doesn't go away.

I feel tired and I lay my head back on the chair. This is what I am learning. To rest when weary. To stop eating when full. To walk away when saturated. I am learning to hear myself. I remember words written by Keith Miller: "The saints were not people with the greatest education or even the largest results. But they did have a couple of traits in common which were almost invisible: what they *said* correlated almost one hundred percent with what they *were* and what they *did*. ... An amazing and invisible power may be released when a person's words and his inner self finally match."

It's surprising to me that having reached so far inside of myself to wrestle with the death of my family, I still missed so much truth. Or maybe I saw the truth, but didn't understand how delicate it is, and how generously it must be fed. In the hours before Beth's birth I so clearly heard God say, "Want me more than you want anything." But hearing it and believing it were not enough. I had to follow it up with my life.

In time it was less difficult to breathe, and I gradually began to anticipate resuming my life. I responded to invitations to speak only after prayer, and I gathered around me a group of prayer partners who would hold me accountable. When I left for my first trip after being bedridden for so long, I still felt poorly, yet we all concurred that it seemed to be the right thing to do. I arrived a day early, and the morning I was to speak I was up for an hour when I suddenly realized that I was well. From that moment the illness was behind me. But now there were many invitations which I did not feel led to accept or for which I felt the timing was not right. I took great pains to listen and to honor this inner guidance. My months in bed had given me permission to let the lives of others be their own. Now I faced the challenge of being well, and still as wise.

Four

THE OBVIOUS PERSONS TO QUESTION about life passages are those who have gone ahead of us. Our grandparents, great-grandparents, the elders. I never knew my paternal grandfather, and my paternal grandmother spoke no English. My maternal grandfather was said to be as fine a person as anyone knew. But he died when I was barely four years old, and all my memories are sketchy. It is only my maternal grandmother whom I remember, and with whom we even lived for the first four years of my life. Throughout my childhood she visited us often, and I have vivid memories of seeing her at her place of work. She ran a small city tea room at a time when women hardly worked at all, let alone managed a business. She was spit-fire, and I admired her initiative.

But when she died in her eighty-third year and the family met to capture her essence for the minister's benefit, I was stunned with an awareness that we barely knew her at all. We knew, of course, names, dates, and places. We knew amusing anecdotes and significant moments. But we didn't know *her*. She hadn't let us in. She died with her story. No one could say what her true feelings, needs, and loves were. That impacted me like a blow to my person. To have lived and died and to never have been deeply known. To have always been proper and right, but to never have shared your dreams, hopes, and hurts. Your acquired wisdom.

So in June of 1986 when my late husband's family announced a large family reunion, I was particularly eager to attend. It would be wonderful for Beth to find her roots and meet relatives face to face. But good for me also. I wanted to hear the stories told by those with the experience of years.

June 1986, Age 38

Midnight. We'll leave for the family reunion in Michigan tomorrow, but tonight we've come here to our beach cottage. It feels good to be back by the water. Immediately I feel calmer, and slower. At 10:30 p.m. when the other beach lovers head back to their cottages, I take a cup of soup to warm my hands and stretch out on my back on the cool sand. The black night sky is a part of me. Even though I'm tired from the rush of packing, this hour of star-gazing is important. If I dismiss the earth, I think I dismiss pieces of my soul.

I tell the stars that I am setting out on this trip with deep emotion. I have fought this awareness until tonight, but with sudden tears, the feelings come. Traveling back to Michigan and Roy's family is a bittersweet reminder of the life which was almost mine. The knowledge still sears, even after eleven years. The last time I made this journey, Roy and Sarah were with me. It seems like it was another lifetime.

My new life, my "today" life is populated with new friends and new circles. I keep moving forward. But now I prepare to drive back into a circle which is filled with reminders and memories. I drive back to a land of mirrors, which will show me what I have lost and what is true: I had to go on alone. Will the experience be happy? Sad? Will there be a gift in the memories for me?

This morning we drive toward Albany, uncomfortable in the suffocating humidity. Beth is edgy and my sister, Beverly, who is journeying with us, is a saint at attempts to keep Beth occupied. When we stop early for the night we are all relieved. Beth and I are in the motel pool three minutes after checking in, and the cool water works miracles on my tightened muscles and tattered nerves. Apart from the strain of driving, I know I am tense as I allow myself to remember the dream Roy and I held for our family and our lives together. I feel so much older tonight than when I originally dreamed that dream. The young bride I was seems sweet, but far away. She was selfish and impatient and innocent. She had fire and hopes. She even thought she had the answers and she had control. I smile, thinking about her. Perhaps she's a large part of who I'm going back to see. Where is she now? And what will it be like to find her?

Niagara Falls has captured us, so we spend a second day there. The power of the water runs through me and we laugh at our wet faces and hair as we ride the boat which takes us to the very foot of the thundering falls. Beth is also fascinated by the strings of museums catering to the unusual and the bizarre. We try our hand at gallery games, and decide that the staggering height of the largest Ferris wheel in North America is for braver souls.

Now we're in the Midwest riding through endless miles of farmland. Green. Rich. Hill upon hill. It is in such contrast to the East coast and its miles of neon fast food signs and prominent billboards. There I live with daily traffic and intrusive sounds. But in these flat stretches of corn and sugar beets there is stillness. We drive along in silence and feast upon the land. Acres of alfalfa offer purple blossoms to the morning, and I think about the genealogy of this earth, and the days when it was well tended and respected. I am reading *Cry, the Beloved Country,* and Paton's words haunt me. "Destroy the land and man is destroyed."

For me, even more troublesome than the fact that we destroy the land is the embarrassing truth that we have destroyed it casually. We are capable of abusing what should be respected, and doing so without conscience. What did the land know that it can now no longer teach?

We arrive. I first spot my sister-in-law, Charlene, and even though it's been eleven years since we've seen one another, the bond of family covers the distance of the years. The belonging is there. We are quickly surrounded by cousins, aunts, and uncles. Some I remember, but many faces are new. I struggle to relate fathers to daughters, nieces to aunts. The strength of heritage is moving. There are so many countries and continents and races. But among them are generations who speak my name and recognize me. I let the feeling of family enfold me. We find Aunt Jane and Uncle Urey, whose spirits have supported me through all my pain. It is a real homecoming, and I drink in their love. They believe in me, and that gift has called me forth. From the center of the commotion Beth announces, "I have *millions* of cousins!" She is so excited. Yet when we gather to watch slides which chronicle the family history, Beth goes off with her Uncle John to the gymnasium to learn how to take foul shots and dribble. I understand. At ten years of age, this reunion is only a summer trip and a chance to be with her grandparents. When she's forty she may have a different perspective. It is sobering to realize that *I'll* be the generation of elderly aunts by then, hoping someone will listen to my story. I will then be the generation who has "gone before." It makes me more determined to listen to the wisdom that surrounds me. It is the greatest thing we pass on.

This morning we have an adult Bible class, and I sit listening to cousin Don Starr's lesson, moved as much by his rich, deep voice as by his words. He quotes Emily Dickinson, reciting,

A Death blow is a Life blow to Some...

Emily's words are passionate, and they affect me. I have lived them. I was jarred into life by death.

Afterward, Don says to me, "We choose whether or not we'll be free." I think about those words all day. Recognizing my interest, he tells me some of his story. We have both buried daughters. I ask what he has learned about freedom, and he says it demands not that we "have" nothing, but that there is nothing we cannot give up. He has no idea what it means to me to meet someone else who has walked on a similar path and has not chosen anger.

In the evening I listen to the family history, lovingly presented by Marilyn Starr. By studying our links, it is easy to identify certain traits which have endured through the generations. Genetic predispositions. Strengths. Weaknesses. But what intrigues me the most is the heart and will of these generations. The death blows, for them, which became blows of life. How they have loved, and when they first understood the truth about living. What binds them. What binds me. They tell their stories. They remember their spartan existence at the turn of the century. I finger an apron crocheted by Beth's great-grandmother Harriet Louise. Who will finger my handwork, in turn? How will my life be re-called? And how will they tell about my broken dreams? Will someone know that I eventually learned we are all filled with *many* dreams, waiting to be given life? Will they say I discovered that it is the *dreaming* which is important, not necessarily the outcome?

In a quiet moment I take out my dream from yesterday and look at it. And I see that it is gone. It has been replaced. It became something new, and I know that is good. I am learning to walk the path I am on, not the one which is behind me, or the one which lies ahead.

I watch Beth as she swims in the gymnasium pool. Her body will change over the years, but she will always be herself. The little girl who surfaces from the water today will always be with her. Hidden from sight, perhaps, but real and vital. Beth will simply grow and mature around the child. But the child will not vanish. It cannot. It is real. The elders sitting with me at the poolside are equally the young children they once were, only now their matured bodies have grown close around them. But inside are the child and the memories. The young bride I once was is also real. She is there within me, somewhere. I do not have to let go of *her*, only her dreams. If I won't let go of her dreams, she will be in control of me, condemning me to past moments of pain. But in allowing her dreams to move and change, I will free us both. I did not know this so clearly when I came. I have learned it by watching the elders and listening to their stories. I see who is bound to the past and who is free. They have taught me a great lesson.

Packing up. I have loved these days and these farm families. I envy their knowing of the earth, its rhythms and cycles. They understand that the long fields of sugar beets and soy are life. It surprises me that nature is such a clear reflection. Embrace the land and it will feed you and teach you. Embrace all the stages of your life and they will do the same. Just do not stand still, clinging. Nothing in nature stands still. Creation is always moving. The teaching is powerful.

Five

OR THE REST OF THE 1980s I explored. I experienced myself at midlife and Beth as a teenager. I studied the Bible, Western religions, Eastern religions, Native American traditions, and Judaism. I could not read quickly enough, and everything became a source of learning. I struggled with great sincerity to let my childhood ideas about God expand and grow up, as I had. I had been taught that specific interpretations of God were the only ones which were correct. Yet God had already revealed himself to me far apart from those slim definitions. In many places where my religious programing insisted issues were black or white, I kept finding a great Mystery. The old, narrow, and certain understandings were no longer big enough to contain this incredible, loving Spirit.

I began to ask myself how we could learn all the things God wanted to teach us if we limited our intake with fear. I saw fear everywhere: the common fear of having to think in a new way; fear of listening to other spiritual points of view; fear of new revelations about God that didn't fit comfortably with existing ideas and opinions. Could the God of all creation really only be capable of revealing himself to all people in one way? I thought a great deal about those disciples who responded when they heard the words of Jesus, "Come, follow me." I thought about them because I was hearing the same voice say the same words. The original followers didn't know where that voice would take them, and neither did I. And clearly, if fear had ruled them, they wouldn't have gone at all.

I read about God as masculine. God as feminine. God speaking boldly. God in the stillness. God seemed to change or move each time I decided I understood too securely who he was. Increasingly I saw the holy in the ordinary and the sacredness of all creation. Truth kept appearing in unexpected corners, and I was often moved to the point of tears by all I saw. I, who once wept in such desperate pain, was now weeping at all the beauty before my eyes. The love of God raced ahead of me, and I could hardly take in its depth and breadth. Still, for all I was seeing, I knew I was seeing only a fraction of what is there. I was getting a glimpse. A shadow. We all see through the glass darkly.

September 1988, Age 40

Today I picked up a book to read entitled *The Quest*. It intrigues me, especially this line: "Grave mistakes that take place in life are made when a person does not follow his heart. When the heart is followed, we touch the Creator." I'm not used to thinking of my heart as being so helpful, or maybe necessary. The God of my childhood required sacrifice and the denial of feelings. But what if that dictate was misguided and needs to be expanded? Something inside knows that's the case and that it's time. Something calls me to get to the God of my maturity and to let the God of my childhood grow.

Yesterday's mail brought a local Adult Education catalog, which describes an introductory talk and several evening classes for those interested in making a wilderness retreat. The experience will include a three-day solo fast in the wilderness, which ends with a night-long vigil on the third evening. The fine print says this will appeal to those seeking guidance and inner vision through spending time alone with God in nature. Literally, it's a Vision Quest. I will at least go to the introductory talk. It's not that spending three days alone outside is the least bit appealing to me. It's that *in spite of* that fact, I feel very compelled by the idea.

The introductory talk is tonight. All the way down the hall to the classroom I ask myself, "What are you doing here?" But I keep walking. I want to grow. I want my knowing of God to grow. About fifty other people, mostly men, have already filled the room. Where are the women? Is it the thought of three nights alone outside that keeps them away? Who am I kidding? I feel paralyzed by the thought myself, plus I hate to feel hungry and I have never fasted before. Still, I am unable to leave my chair.

As the teachers speak it becomes clear that I am not alone in feeling fear. Even the men admit they are afraid. Many are skilled campers and some have fasted before, but it is still different to intentionally go off alone and use a set amount of time, and a particular place, in order to look within yourself and just be alone with God. Outside. That's the killer. Outside. I listen to what is being said, but I don't know if I can do it. I will have to push past fears of the dark, the outdoors at night, insects, animals, hunger.... This is a long list. How can I feel simultaneously drawn to be here, and yet so afraid?

Our homework assignment is to think yourself through a typical day. What things do you always do in the same way and at the same time? Things you do so regularly that you do them unconsciously. I start thinking about that. Nature is always changing, the teachers said, but the same could not be said of me. I drive daily to the same store by the same route to purchase groceries. I don't even want to think about the sameness of most of those groceries. I also walk in the same park, using the same trail, even though there are many choices. It grows worse. I change bed linens on the same day. I eat the same few foods for break-fast. In fact, I *eat* breakfast whether I'm hungry or not. Suddenly I see how much of my life is automatic and unthinking. With a universe of smells and tastes and roads to explore I have this tiny routine. And because it *is* my routine, after a while I go through the day without seeing anything.

I resolve to begin to open my eyes and pay attention. I will pretend I am a tourist in my everyday world. Within hours I am aware of my blind spots...the people in groups whom I never see...the conversations and stories I never really hear. The fringe voices and fringe people. What a terrible awareness. I see how I scan my landscapes once, for the first time. But I never see differently in succeeding looks. I see what I noticed the first time and miss exactly what I missed. Making a conscious effort to see differently is quite an effort. I wonder, do thinking and emotions also take the same blind pathways and find their ruts? What would it take to see the world as brand new? Are there also pathways and ruts in the spiritual world?

Well, if it's a new vision I'm seeking, I guess I've already had my first one. I see how I am lured by the security and comfort of a routine. The physical routine of how I do things and get places, but equally important, the emotional routine of who I've decided I am and how I've decided I'll always react to events. Safe in my little rut, I've become blind to the possibilities of my life. What ruts or routines or expectations of myself and others can I break? I need to look at how I spend my time on a daily basis. How I react when I'm upset.

Or frustrated. Or angry. Maybe I need to let go of some of my ways so there will be room to let in something new. Maybe I need to let go of some of my ways because they simply don't work for me. Human beings are so funny. We'll have first-hand evidence that a certain behavior doesn't bring us the desired results, but we'll never think of changing ourselves or trying something different. I am so guilty of this.

Tonight I read some thoughts written by Henri Nouwen. He says that the Latin word for obedience means "to listen." He also suggests that God, as lover, calls us to unpredictable places. What meaning that holds for me as I buy a tent and air out a sleeping bag in preparation for my days away. Fear still dominates my mood.

The class of fifty has been smaller each week. After each homework assignment (fast for half a day and keep a journal of your experience, spend a day entirely alone, be outside in nature for twelve hours) fewer people return. At the last class there were six of us. I have avoided every homework assignment but the first one. I feel like a fraud. But I am too hungry to fast, too scared of nature and very sure that being alone will be easy. I've been alone a lot. So I listen to everyone else's journal entries and save my experiences for the "real thing." I know this is pathetic, but it's the best I seem able to do. I read more Nouwen and am thinking hard about these lines: "... We make many attempts to establish the outer world as a safe haven ... instead of finding a safe haven within and bringing that to the outer world." I flip through a magazine and read that to "hunt power, you must go into the woods in your own life. You must consciously avoid doing things you are comfortable with; you must break your routines. ..." I may be studiously avoiding my preparations for this adventure, but life is presenting me with the issues whether I am willing or not. I think much of this journey will be about leaving my parent's vision, society's vision — everyone else's vision — and finding my own.

Winter 1989

Today I called Laity Lodge in Leakey, Texas, to make an unusual request. Even though my class of four (two more defaults) is preparing to go together, with the teachers, to quest for vision in Wyoming, I continue to feel strongly directed to spend my wilderness time in a particular Texas canyon that I love. The inner insistence to do it this way will not go away, so I follow my own guidance. Isn't that what this is all about? I ask the retreat center director if I may "use" their canyon for seven days in May when they are not in session. The land will be deserted and there is no place on earth more beautiful or comforting to me than those Texas hills. They answer "Yes" and further make available a cottage named Lode Star where I can orient myself for two days before and after my wilderness time. I take a deep breath and order my airline tickets.

May 1989

I sit on the plane heading toward Texas and my hands are trembling. My heart pumps at twice its normal rate. What is my fear? It takes too much energy to get quiet and name it. I have to use my energy to breathe. I do know that I hate the waiting. I wish the tent were already set up and I was in it. I wish the quest had already begun. Do I live this way a lot? Ahead? This very moment is the only reality. I try to pull myself back.

Breakfast trays are wheeled down the aisle. Will I be able to eat? My stomach is so filled with fear, how could there be room for food? I feared this morning that I would sleep through the alarm. I feared I would be late arriving at the airport and miss the flight. When I wasn't late I feared that since I had made the plane, my baggage wouldn't. Then I happened to see my baggage being loaded right onto my plane, and I immediately changed my fear to one that the baggage will surely be lost when I make my connection in Dallas. I sicken myself. Is this really a picture of me?

My prayer group are all praying for me. I feel Hazel's spirit especially, sure and strong. She sends me a spirit of calm, if only I could receive it. I read the prayer she has given me to take along.

> *Go, When the morning shineth*
> *Go, When the noon is bright*
> *Go, When the eve declineth*
> *Go, When the high of night*
> *Go with pure mind and feeling*
> *Fling earthly cares away*

And in Thy chamber kneeling
Do Thou, in secret, pray.

I will pin this prayer inside my tent. It helps.

What do I fear? I'm not certain my greatest fear is the hunger, although I've said that to many people. I'm not sure it's the long days — or the fear of the night. I may be lonely at times, and scared in the dark. But I will endure it I think. I suspect the great fear is about the unknown. I'm going off alone, to meet the wilderness and look at my life. And I will bring nothing with me to defend me. Not my house, the dollars in my wallet, my friends, my educational degrees. Those will all be useless there. I will be naked. There will be nothing in between me and God.

A stewardess interrupts my thoughts to explain the safety devices aboard the aircraft. Safety? Flying into the upper atmosphere in this machine is an act of faith. How is it safe? I look at my seat belt. Sixteen inches of nylon strapping. It can hold me into this seat, but can it truly protect me? I have this image of all the violent forces of the universe poised against me, and my seat belt matched against them, like Excalibur. It does make me laugh. I think of the way that I live. Carrying keys and locking up my possessions, over and over again. Locking my car. Locking away jewelry. Alarm systems against intruders. Does it all make me safe? Not if the greatest enemies really are within. Maybe I've spent forty-one years fortifying the wrong fortress.

I check my watch. Friends should be waking up now. They will remember me and pray. I think of Beth, snug in her bed, soon to face her small universe of school books, teachers, and lessons. I imagine her walking toward the bus stop, and smile. We are all on adventures. And even miles above the earth, the love of family and friends finds me. The pilot announces that we are flying from Boston to Texas via Canada. I shake my head. This journey is already out of my hands. South, in Native tradition, is the direction of innocence and trust. Do I have things to learn about trust that I don't even guess?

Lode Star. I'm here. My baggage made it and I made it. I spend all afternoon until sunset looking for the right place to carry out this quest, but I can't find a place which seems like "my spot." I consider one clearing where a cactus is in full, brilliant bloom. I love the yellow blossoms, but nothing else about the area feels right. While hiking I find a buzzard's feather and a stone shaped like a dove. I bring both of them back to Lode Star with me. Twice while hiking I encountered deer, and my heart raced. A hawk circled my head and continued to fly above me as I walked. I wondered if his presence was a greeting. Or blessing.

Now I sit on the porch at Lode Star and hold the buzzard's feather in my hand, wondering why it was on my path. The thinking I've done about sameness and routines has sharpened my attention. My teachers also advised us that many things may come to teach us. Even a feather? How? All day as I searched for my place I considered the fact that the wilderness I am really here to explore is within me. I hardly know my own terrain. I've lived for forty-one years looking in other directions.

When you quest for new vision, something will be left behind and something gained. What do I want to leave behind? "My grief" is what comes quickly to mind. I feel ready to operate out of a new consciousness. I also remember the teacher's advice to make fear your ally. He said that fear teaches you self-awareness and self-respect. That's difficult to understand, but I keep repeating it to myself. Lean *into* your fear, not away. Make fear your ally.

I wonder what the fasting will be like? In my twelve-hour "practice" fast I was astonished at my reactions and feelings. Knowing that I was beginning a fast, I immediately felt unsafe and ravenously hungry. Then I began to see how much time I spend with food. My day is organized around it: preparing it, eating it, or thinking about eating it. Food makes me feel safe. I never knew that before. Apparently I eat regularly, regardless of appetite. That day of my "practice" fast I gave up after thirty minutes.

If I feel pangs of hunger when I can't possibly be hungry, then what am I hungry for? What is food trying to fill? Maybe I won't be able to do this quest after all. I'm afraid I'll fail in some way. I won't do it perfectly or get it right. These doubting voices are so me. I have to repeat to myself that I will do this the way I do it. And I believe God will honor me, however that is. I don't want "doing this perfectly" to become my focus. I want to accept myself as I am. Consciously or unconsciously I have set my house in order as if I may never return. My bills are paid, my desk clear. All my correspondence is up to date. I have prepared for the death of whatever in me needs to die before something new can be born. I think I am ready.

Sunday

Tomorrow it all begins. I feel very frightened, and the fear fills me enough to even keep away my hunger. I, who am always hungry. I sit on the porch at Lode Star and notice that I am chilly in the midday heat. I try to have a time of worship, facing the hills. I read Psalm 8 and cry. I want to read "I will lift up mine eyes unto the hills," and simply cannot remember what psalm it is. I know it as well as my name, but still can't think of it. I observe how fear apparently affects memory and thinking.

My right eye hurts and is somewhat swollen. Maybe it's infected. Will I be okay? Is something terrible going to happen to it and I will be all alone and without help? Will this cancel my quest? Do I secretly wish it would? I take a deep breath. Maybe it's even important to my quest. I am seeking new vision and my eye responds. Perhaps it tells me that this is where I am wounded: my seeing is not clear.

A truck pulls into the driveway and it's Eddie. It feels so good to see a friend. The final hour of the weekend retreat at Laity Lodge is beginning. Then everyone will leave the canyon. Before going home he thought

I might like to pray with someone. He has never been more right. He reads from Isaiah 43:18, 19:

> *Do not call to mind the former things,*
> *Or ponder things of the past.*
> *Behold I will do something new,*
> *Now it will spring forth;*
> *Will you not be aware of it?*
> *I will even make a roadway in the wilderness,*
> *Rivers in the desert.*

I read Hazel's poem and a verse by T. S. Eliot:

> *We shall not cease from exploration*
> *And the end of all our exploring*
> *Will be to arrive where we started*
> *And know the place for the first time.*

We wonder aloud what I'll find, and in silence we break bread and drink cups of juice. I am fully present in the moment, so it is truly worship.

Eddie gives me a map of the terrain, and when the canyon is empty I hike west of Lode Star, still searching for my spot. Some of the way is steep, but after an hour's hike I find a clearing circled by bushes of violet sage. From this spot I can see the river. There is a feeling of recognition. This is the place where I will wait with God. For safety, I will carry a walkie-talkie which will be monitored by Laity employees who live a few miles away. They have already sat down with me to talk about wildlife in the area and any potential dangers. I guess I am as prepared as I will ever be. I walk back to Lode Star wondering what the hike will feel like tomorrow when I have jugs of water and my sleeping gear to carry.

It's evening and I sit outside to watch the sunset. A small green insect sits with me for over two hours, hugging the rim of the chaise cushion. Is he sleeping? Waiting? Whatever, he is in no hurry. Maybe that's the message. A hummingbird sucks nectar from a nearby flower. I can barely believe the volume of his hum. He's like a small motor. I have never noticed a hummingbird before.

I took my watch off a day ago, so I have no idea what time it is except by watching the sun. I am still barely hungry. I think about going inside to get a muffin, but then hear my stomach asking why I would do that if I'm not hungry. It is remarkable to observe how food has become a habit I use to fill empty time and space.

And it's good to already be so quiet that I can know this. Instead of eating, I go to bed.

Monday

Dawn. This is it. I wake at dawn and want to sleep. No one will ever know when (or if) I leave Lode Star. Why not get a long rest? I peek out the window and the words of Hazel's prayer keep returning to me: "Go, when the morning shineth." A fly circles my head mercilessly. Two nights ago, my first night at Lode Star, I woke up in the middle of the night hearing my name spoken. I wasn't frightened by that. It felt like an affirmation that I've been called here. This trip is not "my" idea. God has beckoned me to follow him into the wilderness and to trust that I will be protected. Why does he spend time caring about my one small life? I don't know. But he does draw me. Suddenly I have this deep awareness of myself as a soul who is being led somewhere. I get up out of bed and prepare to go.

As I begin to collect my gear I realize that getting to my spot is going to be very difficult. I foolishly refused a friend's offer of a backpack. I must have thought I was superwoman. Now as I stare at my tent, sleeping bag, water jugs, and pack I see the full consequence of my pride. There will be no way to do this in one trip. I have two hands and three loads. This journey will have to be made in stages. Great. I will have plenty of time to think about how I refuse help. I am seeing myself already.

I start off, taking a third of my items a quarter of a mile down the dirt road. Then I retrace my steps and bring the second load that far. Finally, the third. I am not going to forget this lesson quickly. At first it is still breezy and pleasant and I compliment myself on the early start. But in no time the level road disappears, I am hiking up vertical terrain, the sun is scorching, and I want to die. I keep at it. As I cross the dam I rest and notice the trees rising out of the water. I look into the water and see how the trees have bonded with the algae and plant life. Aren't I out here to learn how to bond to God? Nature bonds, but it does not cling. I surprise myself by saying that out loud. It's a sudden observation. I look at the trees for a long while.

As I watch I begin to see that everything around me — the trees, rocks, river, flowers — everything is simply and profoundly yielded. With that knowing comes a wave of peace. The earth is yielded to God. The inner calm unlocks my memory. "I will lift up mine eyes unto the hills" is Psalm 121. I read it before going on and weep.

Back to work. I cannot believe the physical cost of this journey. It feels like 103 degrees, even in the shade. I am soaked to the skin with perspiration, exhausted, hungry, and still not there. Not nearly there. This three-time repetition of every step I take is killing me. It makes the road seem endless. I want to scream in frustration. I am ready to forget everything and go back.

Then it occurs to me that maybe this awful struggle is actually an important lesson. I let my heart open and listen. Aren't I feeling, with every footstep, what every man and woman feels when they are called to achingly repeat the same tasks day after day? I put down my tent and sleeping bag and retrace my steps to pick up my jugs of water. I am the migrant worker in the fields, picking beans, or the teacher repeating the same lectures while few pay attention. I get the water jugs to their destination and walk back a third time to get my pack. I am on an auto assembly line, or a parent getting up in the middle of the night for a crying child. The same task. Again. And again. In my bones and in my blisters I feel the weight of obedience to the sameness which is unavoidable in all our lives. I am dripping in sweat, the ankle splint from a recent sprain cuts into me...but my skin is alive with a taste of my brothers' and sisters' burdens. I see that we are not separate, and their faithfulness moves me to tears.

And then, in a single moment, I am flooded with love. Suddenly I "feel" the love God has for all people as we live out our insignificant lives and perform our routine tasks. Compassionate, warm, tender love pours down on me and washes over me. I cannot explain it, but it is real and so tangible that it begins to lift me. I am still tired and hungry and doubtful of ever reaching my spot, yet this love picks me up and I am in its grip. I see how God honors simple obedience to our smallest tasks. I feel love all over me. Ahead of me. Behind me. Above me. Beneath me. I feel it in the wind. There is no way not to be affected by such a power. I continue my tiresome, trudging trek. But it now has become almost a dance. A gift I give. The voice which says, "Come into my wilderness" is more loving than any I have ever known.

I reach my spot and pitch the tent. Before coming I obsessed about the possibilities of cold and rain, never giving a thought to heat and wind. Naturally that's what I'm suffering with now. The heat is oppressive, and the wind blows so hard I'm not sure the tent will stay up. I am also feeling bored, something I cannot believe. Boredom never happens to me. But I am feeling bored and alone and would give anything for some human companionship. In spite of what I've already experienced, I feel uninterested now in learning more, in observing nature — in anything. I can't seem to get settled and I wish this were over. I keep thinking that what I really want is food.

Nature is noisy. The birds and insects never stop their calling and cawing. Even the wind has a sound. I never noticed that before. Why is all of creation singing? I see nothing to sing about right now.

I am lonely and I feel depressed. I can't believe myself as I write this. I am used to loving my aloneness, not to missing people. As I write, a brilliant red bird flies by and takes my breath away.

I feel angry at my campsite. How dare it be so distant, so remote, so apart. I thought I'd love it, but I hate it. Lode Star feels like a distant planet. I could just get up and return there. I could be feasting on fruit and muffins. Maybe I really won't last through this.

I stare at a tree. A tree alone, *all* alone, couldn't make it. It has to have soil and sunlight and rain. If it's true in nature, it must be true for me. I couldn't make it all alone. I am interconnected and I need others for my survival. Is that why I feel so wretched now? I'd rather have the fear back, because compared to this terrible loneliness fear looks good. I feel as if someone has taken a baseball bat and slugged me in the chest. I ache with being alone.

God, what is this about? If I know how much I need others, doesn't that lead me to cling *more* and not less? Or are you trying to show me that the deep need I feel for others isn't bad...the issue is *how* the need gets filled. Clinging will not fill the need. It will only fill the space. If I don't cling, will you care for me just as you care for the tree?

I sigh. I am always afraid I will not be taken care of, so I try to satisfy my needs before I truly feel them. I am afraid that if *I* don't orchestrate this, my needs won't be met. I run my hand over the rocky soil at my feet. It occurs to me that my need for connectedness is as old as the earth. God, are you the only one who will ever completely satisfy the longing inside of me? Will every other person, place, and thing fall short? Will my clinging take me in the wrong direction? Should I be more like the tree, yielded to you? Trusting. And if I am, will you respond?

I think this is the longest day of my life. Eighty-nine hours have surely passed, but I can tell by the sun that it is only a little past noon. My mind continues to struggle. If the point is to yield to God, then why bond to others at all? How does it benefit me? As I ask the question a flock of birds fly in V-formation over my head. A family of deer scamper through the bushes. They remind me that I am not a single soul. I am part of a whole creation of relations. It affects the birds if two of them leave the V-formation. The safety of the deer is compromised if one or two deer leave their habitat. It is not different for me. My choices have meaning for others, too. If I lived in that consciousness, I know I would weigh all my words and actions differently. I am not used to thinking of myself "in relation" beyond my family and community. I think I am able to do things which affect no one but me.

I am staring at the river thinking that I would give anything for the sound of a human voice. I watch the water and think of letting love flow through me, instead of trying to hold on to it. The supply is from God. There will be enough. I hear rustling in the leaves behind me and brace myself for an encounter with a large animal. I turn slowly and look over my shoulder. It *is* an animal, but a human one. He draws closer and I see his blue shirt and the name "Gabe" written over his pocket. My first reaction is despair. A quest is supposed to be solitary, and if I interact with someone, mine will be spoiled. I am still agonizing when his voice, still several feet behind me, says, "Hello."

Gabe is employed by Laity Lodge and is responsible, with others, for the care of the grounds. Aware that a woman was camping alone out here, he felt led to check on me. For a while he too silently watches the river, still staying several feet behind me. Finally he says, "God is all around you here. *Everywhere.*"

Softly I reply, "Yes, I know."

But obviously I don't know. At least not fully enough. If I did know there would have been no need for God to send this man to assure me. He waits a while longer and I hope he doesn't see my tears. The power of everything is amplified in these woods. The beauty of human contact. My recognizing my need for it. God's mysterious supplying of it. His taking care of me. It's almost more than I can contain. As I fight to control my emotions Gabe says, "Is the walkie-talkie they gave you working?"

Why would he ask that question? In fact, it isn't. It was the first thing I tested when I got to my spot. "No," I say.

"I suspected that," he replies. I can't even entertain the origin of his suspicion. His knowing. I am fighting hard for control as it is. He walks toward me and hands me *his* radio which does work, and walks quietly away.

After he leaves I can't stop crying. I weep because God has just demonstrated that he will take care of me. I weep because he treats me so gently. I weep because he knows me by name. I weep because birds are dancing in circles over my head, showing me that there is nothing greater to do than join the lovesong of creation. I see that this quest of mine is being designed by God in great detail. The book says the quest must be solitary. God thought otherwise. He gave me what I needed.

The red bird sings at my feet as I drink water for my dinner. It is enough.

As darkness approaches I notice that one of the trees behind me is half-living and half-dead. I wonder why, and inwardly hear the tree explain that she divided against herself. I think about the voices of criticism I often listen to inside my head. But I never thought about the consequence of listening to them. Do they divide me?

This day feels so endless. The time won't pass. It inches along, just to torture me. I've felt so much loneliness today. Partly loneliness for people, but more so inner loneliness, I think. The Gethsemane place. For a while I felt so depressed I wanted to leave. I keep wondering if I am doing it right, which implies, I guess, that I think there is a right way to do it. That's definitely a Paula thought. I feel hungry and weak and I keep thinking there are two more days and nights ahead of me. God help me. Right now I am weary in every way.

Night comes. I watch the river being soothed by the wind. I feel physically weak and tired, but inwardly strong, if that is possible. I'm learning the depth of some needs I hadn't even named or fully recognized. And I'm awed at the way the earth is teaching me about the interconnectedness of all things.

I was afraid of the cold, and I've been baked in heat. I was afraid of big, creepy, crawly bugs and it's been fire ants, a millimeter in length, which have gotten my attention.

I feared rain, thunder, and lightning, and have only felt the wind as my constant companion. I also feared the day would never end.

But now, at last, it has.

Tuesday

I see a yellow butterfly this morning, and wonder what message she may have for me. "Be cheerful," she seems to say with her flight.

My scarlet bird is so beautiful I ache when he flies by. He is with me all the time. Last night I watched hundreds of ants. They moved so fast it was incomprehensible. They darted in a long line, to and fro, like traffic on a freeway. What was their project? I had no idea, but they surely did. They unerringly followed some instinct, and their pattern was precise. I couldn't help but think what a gift it must be to know so truly the purpose for which you exist.

I am noticing that the bees never, ever quit. Late at

night, early in the morning, their drone goes on and on. They drive me crazy because they are such a mirror of me. I want to yell at them, "Give it up, will you? Relax!" In sublime contrast, the buzzards and hawks just float and dance all day long. All they seem to do is play. They know *how* to play. God, make me more like a bird in flight.

Yesterday I feared the night more than anything, and it was the night which turned out to be glorious. The stars were brilliant and so close...like crystal beams. It was new to sleep under their canopy. The moon's brightness actually distracted me from sleep. It pierced the night sky with glory. Then the lightning bugs came out and were a mini-fireworks display. I couldn't believe their size, their number, or their brilliance. I felt as if a light show was being put on for me, personally. The earth is so beautiful.

When darkness did finally come, I had no fear. There was a fly in my tent, and I spent several minutes of frustration trying to shoo him out. Then I considered that perhaps he'd been sent to be my companion. I stopped swatting at him, thanked him for his presence, and asked him to please not pester me. What would anyone think, if I told them this? I was trying to communicate with a fly. But the fact is that he never flew near me again, and I did feel strangely comforted that he was there. I no longer felt alone.

I laugh at how this must sound. A fly is certainly small protection against the possible terrors of the night. But I am a student here. I am learning, not directing. And that fly assured me of my safety. Once or twice I did hear rustling noises. My heart was beating so fast. But essentially I felt so much a part of the place where I was — so at "one" and in harmony with it — that gradually I relaxed and believed that any creatures roaming around nearby were there to protect me, not attack. I fell asleep saying, "Thank You."

I'm amazed that I have already gone twenty-four hours without food and I am still managing. I am definitely weaker than I was yesterday, but so much more in harmony with myself. I hope I never take food for granted again. I've never thought about this before, but other species — plants, animals, fish — really do offer their lives for ours to go on. I have my morning communion of water with a lizard who is resting beside me. My offering to God is my gnawing hunger and my fatigue.

How well you are caring for me in this wilderness,

God. My preparations and fears were far worse than this reality. You are gentle and have reached down and blessed me. And I am only one of millions of your children. Your care humbles me and awes me. By some miracle I see that I truly am in the palm of your Hand.

What is this quest about? I expected severity and am being graced by gentleness. Will I receive any clarity about my life today, or will I still wait and wonder?

I wish I could understand why I so often change myself, trying to please others, and gain their approval of who I am. Right now, the fear of meeting with someone's disapproval seems so small compared to the fears I've had to face to come here and stick it out. Does the river try to please a tree? Does the bird try to please a stone? In nature, things are simply who or what they are. A tree, trying to please the river, would be ridiculous. I imagine a tree trying to edge itself over so it can place shade in a different spot. The notion is silly. But I wonder... isn't that what I do? What if I put all my energy and power into being me, instead of someone else's version of me?

I continue to think that this experience is going too easily. Maybe I'm not doing it right. At least I'm doing it, though. I have to keep reminding myself, there is no set way. There is only mystery and change and what is. My life would be so different if I thought that all of it was an adventure to be carved out and created, with no set way to experience things. Immediately I'd be so much freer.

Every time the red bird sings I feel such joy!

Last night, under the stars, I prayed aloud for many whom I love. I felt their spirits and thanked God for them, one by one. I thought about what it means to drink deeply of all the people in my life, but not to cling to them. I kept remembering the V-formation. As I watch the canyon wren or inspect the improbable flowers blooming in this rocky soil, I hear God saying, "I will supply your needs." I guess I cling to people and things because I do not trust that fully enough. I really don't believe that nothing generates with me, and everything begins and ends with God's bounty. I pray for a new consciousness which knows the truth that none of us are separate and everything comes from God.

Midday. I am hungry and very weary. My stomach is complaining loudly. Yet strangely, I also feel full. I am lying down to keep in rhythm with myself. I don't know if I have ever felt so still, inside and out. Buzzards circle over my head and my scarlet bird makes frequent visits. I look at the bird and think how glorious it would feel to be so free. Bees fly around me, dragonflies hum, lizards creep and crawl near me. But I am not disturbed by them, nor am I afraid. They feel like kin.

I look at the river. If I were to cling to it, I'd have to pick it up in a bucket and take some of it with me. I'd separate it from itself. If I were to cling to a tree, I'd have to break part of it off, or uproot it. If I were to cling to a rock I'd have to remove it from its home. This is worse: if I were to cling to the red bird, I'd have to cage him.

Maybe when I cling to people, I dim them, too. I separate them from their own inner roots. I help them to believe that they are dependent on me, or that the hunger in their bellies is a cry for me. I convince us both. And then we never hear the cry of hunger which is for God. Until this moment I have not understood that. I am hungry for God. I eat and drink and distract myself too much with noise and activity to have ever felt this deeper hunger, but it is there. Now as I am eating and drinking (taking in) God's creation, I feel satisfied. I am letting myself live in its beauty without needing to own it or control it or secure it for tomorrow. I am seeing it as it is ... *really* seeing it. And that is enough, to really see. I am present to this moment. That brings joy. I know why the hawk soars.

God, you really meant creation to be enjoyed, didn't you? That is why so many of your creatures spend their time dancing. Is it the purpose of every tree, every hill, every rock...every soul, to give glory to your ongoing creation? Is that the greatest purpose? Are we often lost in self-serving service in your name when we should be sitting at your feet feeling the sun and learning about beauty from the clouds? Do we miss the song which is always being played?

It is so still. I receive the day.

I reach inside my tent for a water jug and see that the fly has died. My sadness is genuine. I thank him for being with me through my first night. He is not an insignificant insect, as he surely would have been to me two days ago. He is an expression of God. God's creation. I cannot look in any direction without seeing creations of God. Therefore nothing is insignificant, and everything worthy of respect and care. Nothing is second-class. What God has made is of value. In my arrogance as a human being I have dismissed and demeaned the creations of the very God I profess to love. I see my value judgments and my assumed superiority with such clarity, and ask God and his creation to forgive me. The nature I am encountering in this wilderness is my own.

It's midafternoon, I think, and time is starting to stand still again. I'm tired and hungry and can't get comfortable. It's hot. I've lapped some water from the river onto my arms, legs, and face, and it feels good. The heat is sapping my strength. The sun is so far away in the sky, and yet it covers the earth with such intense heat. Its power is staggering, but I know it doesn't begin to equal the full measure of God's power, which fills the universe.

My red bird appears again. He is never far away.

The passage of time is almost as much a challenge as the hunger and being alone. In my usual life there is never enough time. That is a reality I constantly confront. I chase the clock every day. Here, it feels like the Twilight Zone. The minutes each take at least an hour. The afternoons are punishing with their heat. What will it be like tomorrow night when I supposedly stay awake all night? It is unthinkable to do *anything* to lengthen these days. I long for a book to read, but that would only carry me into another world, away from this one. It's impressively hard to live fully present with no people, music, books, telephone, anything to distract me. It's just the inside of me and the reality of God's presence.

The day is finally beginning its metamorphosis into night. The wind changes subtly and the sounds of nature are different. The only being that does not seem to acquiesce to the change is the bee. One still drones above my head. Why, God, are you making me look at myself like this? It's a miserable reflection.

I've been singing hymns I can recall from memory and feeling my hungry stomach. I wish I would have a visit from the red bird. As I just wrote that thought, he appeared! I feel weary. I content myself to be like the trees and just "be." I know I am a sorry sight. My shirt and shorts are filthy and sweat-soaked. One foot is covered with blisters. My hair, if I could see it, must look like a wild mop. It feels like Brillo. My legs are hairy and my teeth need to be brushed. Only God could love me now.

I force myself to walk down the river to watch the reflection of the sunset on the canyon wall. I am lost in that beauty for an hour when three or four flies start buzzing relentlessly around my head, aiming directly for my eyes. Since every insect and creature has treated me so graciously in their world for these two days, I am puzzled by the flies' behavior. I have a feeling they are trying to get me to move. But why? Then I hear it, in the distance. Thunder. The sky I am facing is clear and light-filled. But I get up and turn around, looking at the western sky. One look. I see purple and black clouds and I'm on my feet and running to my tent. My heart is pounding.

What was it Hazel said in prayer group when I expressed my fear of a storm while I was on this quest? Something to the effect that if thunder and lightning came, they would be mighty displays of God's power, but would not harm me. Okay, God, I shout through gulped breaths. I *do* believe in your power. I believe in you. So I don't need a lesson. Skip the storm. I get it! The only answer is a streak of lightning. I leap for my tent and jump inside, pulling my knees to my chest. I recite Scripture: "Do not be anxious for tomorrow, for tomorrow will care for itself. Each day has enough trouble of its own." You're not kidding!

I think about all the times I've worried about pure nonsense. Like rushing to get somewhere on time. Or agonizing over what to wear. Those moments seem insane right now.

I wonder if the deer are afraid, like I am?

There's a huge flash of lightning and the birds start calling frantically. Then in a second they are perfectly silent. What do the animals know? Being zipped up in this tent is starting to feel suffocating. I feel sweaty and scared and smothered by heat. What do I think this nylon is going to protect me from, anyway, except rain? It's hot. If I have to stay here all night I think I can count on sweating my way to a new dress size by morning. I wonder if I'll be alive in the morning?

Suddenly a bright light is circling my tent and I hear a voice calling my name. I don't know if this is wonderful or terrible. I'm alone on this side of the river, four miles away from the nearest person... who can be here? It occurs to me that maybe I've died from fright and this is the famous tunnel. So in answer to, "Paula, are you there?" I squeak out, "Yes." I peak out and see a man's shadow and someone who identifies himself as Ken. I sigh with deep relief. Jesus and the tunnel are postponed. Ken is part of the Laity Lodge team who knows I'm out here. He tells me he's been listening to the weather radar and learned that the fast approaching storm is severe... it carries hail, and sightings of two tornadoes.

"I really don't want to interrupt your time here," he says. "But if the creek and river rise in the storm, you will be completely cut off and no one could rescue you even if they wanted to."

As he talks the lightning and thunder are dancing around us. My heart has wrapped itself around the word "tornado" and I feel like I'm choking. What I want to do is jump into his truck and watch the storm from the safety of his home, or wherever he takes me. But if I do that, I know I'll never return to this wilderness and finish out my quest. For several moments I struggle with my fear, and yet my sense of God's call. I am, after all, in a thirty-five-dollar nylon tent, surrounded by trees. Finally I hear this voice, strangely like mine, proposing a compromise. I know there is an empty bunkhouse three-quarters of a mile away, and I announce that I will go there. This decision seems half-way between giving up and being crazy.

The thunder is increasingly fierce, so I grab water, my journal, and a flashlight and let Ken drive me to the bunkhouse. Once there I ask him what is the safest thing to do if a tornado comes. He tells me to pull a mattress on top of me and jump into the shower stall at the end of the room. "How will I know a tornado is approaching?" I ask. I sound so calm, as if I am asking for directions to City Hall.

"Well," Ken says, "you usually *don't* know. That's the problem. But if you hear the wind start to roar like the sound of a train, that's a fair warning."

I thank him and say goodbye, listening until I hear his truck reach the other side of the river and drive out of the canyon. Then the enormity of my decision really fills me. All help is gone, and I know, as never before, that I am all alone in this canyon.

I sit down on the edge of a bunk suspiciously eyeing the floor for spiders. Now I know I'm mentally ill. I'm alone in the woods, possibly in the path of two tornadoes, and I'm still nervous about a bug. I think of the hymn "How Great Thou Art," and the verse, "I see the stars, I hear the rolling thunder...." What am I doing here? Fears race ahead of me. Is Beth okay? I picture her trusting smile, and in the moment feel unable to protect either of us. Adrenaline surges through my body.

I consider my two days in the wilderness so far. The days have passed slowly, but have been serene. I have been taught lesson after lesson by the creatures in God's kingdom. Where are these friends now? Are the animals safe? Are they afraid, like I am? Where will a small red bird go in this fury? Rain lashes at the windows and the wind is howling. I understand that if anything happens to one of these creatures, it also happens to me. We have been living in communion. I beg God to let the red bird be safe.

The storm worsens. A whippoorwill cries out with a piercing trill. Her song cuts through all the other chilling night noises. The animals' screeches and the wind, rain, and thunder make the night feel wild. The lightning bolts are constant now. And this has all happened within the space of one hour. I think of a loved one who is dying from bone cancer. Is this how he feels? Caught up in a fury. Life changed without notice. His gentle God vanishes and all around is darkness and silence.

"Where are you, God, in this storm?" I ask out loud. Where are you when illness comes? What makes a gentle God suddenly change? How can it seem safe to believe in you when cancer roars through your body and eats your bones. And how can it be safe to follow you and depend on you when the wind is so fierce and the sounds so frightening? Where are you, God? Why can't I feel your presence anymore? Silence.

I feel betrayed. I remember this feeling when Roy and Sarah were killed. I remember trying so hard to find God when only darkness was showing. God, why do you ask us to love you in the dark?

I keep listening for a train roar. I already have a mattress in the shower, ready. The bunkhouse is creaking and I'm so scared I'm shaking. What if the trees start crashing down? What if the windows blow in? There is no sense of God, no sense of my usual faith. All I can feel is the storm. I feel abandoned.

Then I hear a question, deep within me, spoken into the night. "Paula, can you trust me even when you do not feel my presence? Can you trust me when there is no reassurance? Can you believe when you don't understand my ways? Can you get yourself still, and just know that I am there?"

The question overpowers everything. The storm within me becomes quiet and somehow I know that this is the question I have come into the wilderness to answer: *What is greater: my fear or my faith?* Whom or what do I trust most deeply? Do I want my own way, or do I really want God?

I sit for a long while in my inner stillness. I've never experienced anything like the force of this raging wind. The walls seem ready to blow out at any second. Hail the size of a fist pelts the window panes. The sounds are unearthly. But God's question is posed with greater force. Who am I, really? Am I his, or am I pretending? Can I trust, whatever circumstances surround me? What do I really think? *Am I safe, or am I not?*

And quietly, in the midst of the chaos of the night, I find a place of truth at the very core of me. I trust God. I sit for a long while in the silence of that knowing. If I blow away and die tonight, or live and am protected, I am equally safe.

"At the core of me is God." I say it out loud, like a prayer. At the core of me is God. Suddenly I see the fury of the night as startling and beautiful. I am humbled right to my knees, but this time not from fright, but from reverence. I see the same storm through new eyes. I bow my head. "Majestic, mysterious God. Great Spirit, which moves through all things. I will never know you fully. I will always be learning to love you. But *you* are love. I am sure of that. I believe that behind all fury is love. I do not see it or feel it right now. But I trust it is there." And for a long moment I let the trust fill me.

The storm continues. I am increasingly unafraid, but as the air changes I am suddenly shivering with cold. I jump and strain and manage to pull down a dingy window curtain. Pulling it over me, I lie down on the bunk, sliding my journal under my head for a pillow. I have nothing else. I hear the storm, but I breathe deeply and fall into a child's sleep. Nothing disturbs me. I know I am safe.

At dawn I awaken and listen. The storm has passed. The danger is over. I am still shivering with cold, needing a warm sweatshirt. I hope my pack and tent can be found. But nothing will take precedence over running back to the river and waiting in the spot where the red bird comes. I won't be all right until I know he's all right. The woods have taught me that we are all connected as one.

Slowly I put back the window curtain and remove the mattress from the shower stall. Wherever the tornadoes decided to spin, no hair on my head was touched. I pick up my journal, flashlight, and water and push open the creaky bunkhouse door. As I am about to step out, a flash of color at my foot startles me, and I look down. There on the doorstep, waiting, is the red bird. Tears spill from my eyes and I can barely breathe. How could he possibly know where to find me, or that this very doorstep was mine?

We look at one another for a long while. The force of this winged being's presence can never be expressed in words that I know how to shape. But in spite of that, I do not doubt the moment's power or its meaning. The bird and I understand. The storm was one display of power. His waiting for me, another. Such a moment is a gift.

I begin the walk back to my spot and (hopefully) my tent. I have been touched by a power and a tenderness which have thoroughly changed me. I know I must still look like me, but truly, I will never be the same. I walk slowly down the dirt path. I am new.

Wednesday

In forty-eight long hours I have come to know these woods and its creatures. I realize that this quest is almost over. One more day and night. Yesterday I longed for this to be finished; now, inexplicably, I feel like weeping. I know the place at the creek bed where the deer like to cross. I know the circling pattern of the buzzards. And when their pattern changes, like today, I understand that nature is changing. I know the trees where my red bird loves to sing. I know the sounds of the evening, and the panicked sounds of the four-leggeds and the winged creatures. Flies have guided and comforted me. I have been accepted into this habitat. When I leave tomorrow, and then return again someday, will these creatures remember me? I feel safe with these beings. Who will understand this connection I feel?

My little tent survived the storm, sturdy and strong. But the effects of the wind are everywhere. One jug of water tipped over inside the tent, leaving quite a puddle. I say to myself, "I would have been safe if I'd stayed here." I wonder if I should have stayed? I'll never know. I did what seemed right at the time: I tried not to make "staying" more important than listening to my own heart. Listening to my own heart was what I came out here to do. Strangely, I do not feel hungry or weary today. I feel strong.

The day is quiet, almost reverent. It is almost as if the day knows I am preparing myself for an important ceremony, and it is preparing too. I am deeply grateful to nature, which has protected me, instructed me, and watched out for me. It seems to me now even more ludicrous than it always did that we measure off land by plots and think we really own pieces of the earth. I now see that we can pound in hundreds of property stakes and fill file drawers with deeds...but no piece of earth has ever been owned by anyone but God. Even if I pick up a rock and take it home with me, it won't be mine.

The canyon is different today. Still, like me. Perhaps it prays too, preparing itself for my vigil. I will not sit up alone. I haven't seen one fly, and very few insects. The buzzards are perched in trees, not circling. No birds. Even the red bird has been absent since I saw him this morning. I'm trying hard not to be sad.

It's much cooler. I'm wearing long pants, a sweatshirt and a wind parka. The scorching heat is a memory. Nature is showing me all her faces, and the frequency and ease with which she changes. The birds and insects understand, and move with her. I think of what it's usually like for me to change. Only the bee hasn't quit his normal pattern. He's so focused and determined I think he still drones after death.

What I do see today is butterflies. They have circled

me and followed me since early morning. Butterflies are everywhere. I know the butterfly is a symbol of resurrection. Do *they* know their significance, and are they waiting for the death of my old self tonight and the resurrection of someone new?

I drink some water and look hard at my canyon and beloved river. And suddenly, as I'm watching, everything begins to change. It feels as if I am witnessing a scene change. The sun slowly appears for the first time all morning. Clouds roll back. The birds return, except for the red bird, who is still out of sight. The insects find voice and begin to call to one another. I have no words for the sight before me — this coming to life of the canyon. The glory of it. Is this how it will be for me one day? Are they showing me? A hawk takes flight, and I have never seen anything so beautiful.

Afternoon. I have waited for the red bird to appear for hours. I want him to join me. Then it occurs to me that he is a gift. I remember what I've learned. I don't want to diminish his light by filling my own hands. I whisper to his invisible spirit, "Sorry! I'm still learning. Be where you are. Be free. Go!" As I say "Go," he appears, dropping closer to my feet than ever before. He dances and struts on a rock, showing off his fancy feathers. Then with sublime grace he flies off above the trees, a burst of red in the sky.

Evening. My heart is pensive. How will I go back to living, and yet still remember? How will I contain both worlds at the same time? I sit on a stone and thank the river and canyon and everyone for giving to me so richly.

It seems as if it will be a beautiful night. The sky is blue and clear, with only scattered clouds. I sit so peacefully. I've finally run out of things to think and am learning to "be." This has been a harder process than I ever could have imagined. I've never before spent time solely with the inside of me. It was hard work to get to this quiet place. Tomorrow it will be absolutely wonderful to have food, and a book... and *especially* clean clothes and a shower. What joy it will be to get to Lode Star and then to see people. I want to be hugged and held. It will have a meaning it never did before.

Today's sunset is simply stunning. The light on the canyon so soft, the river very still. The trees touch one another but hardly move. The rocks wait for the night. Cactus blossoms are closing and the air is serene. I am so blessed. God has given me beauty, gifts, richness, power, fury, majesty... and right now, peace. If I go back home and forget all I have learned, it is not so much myself that I feel I will be letting down. It is them. The flies and the bee, the river and the red bird...all of them who have worked so hard to open my heart and expand my sight. I never lived inside my own wilderness before, and they are the only companions to that world that I have. They are my sole witnesses. How will I explain to my human world that these creatures have unerringly and purposefully been my teachers? That all of God's creation knows the way to the Kingdom.

People will think I'm crazy. I would too, if I hadn't been here. But it happened to me, and its truth is in me.

I go now to prepare for my night of vigil. I put my journal away. I honor the meaning of this night by recording it only in my memory and my heart.

Thursday

It must be nearly 6:00 a.m. and I am waiting that one, last agonizing hour before the dawn. If I could physically get behind the hills and make the light appear,

I would. I want to get out of here and back to Lode Star. I want to take a shower, read a book, and sit where there are cushions. I want to touch friends and talk to those who love me. I ache for human contact. Endless waiting. And then, there it is. The light has come.

I thank the night and the canyon and everyone. I thank the dawn. I *really* thank the dawn. I empty my remaining water on the soil and thank the earth for protecting me. I scatter the circle of stones I had placed around me, leaving no trace that I've ever been here. The evidence will be inside of me. The first drops of rain begin to fall as I am packing up my tent. But I am so glad to be going back to Lode Star that I don't care about getting wet. I only worry that the stepping stones I need to get me across the creek bed will be too slippery for my passage.

Putting half of my gear under a tree, I head off with the first load. Only two loads for the return trip. The jugs of water are empty. My first trip over the creek bed is okay, but when I make the return trip the rocks are already treacherous. I pick up my remaining gear — the rain is steady now — and walk toward the creek for the second time. I've already said my goodbyes. It's time to go home.

Ten feet down the road a deer stands in my path and never moves, even as I come closer. I think of how trusting these animals have been as I've lived among them. How did they know I was safe? The deer and I look at one another for a long time. I say to him, "Brother." Eventually he turns and I go on my way. When I get as far as the infamous bunkhouse I decide to leave my tent and sleeping bag there until tomorrow. So with just my personal belongings and the camp's walkie-talkie, I head toward the dam and the road to Lode Star. The red bird suddenly flies in front of my feet and I stop and smile. There is great emotion in my heart, but I take no second looks back. I want us both to be free, and I remember what I've learned about clinging. By the time I cross the dam I am wet from head to toe.

Seventy-four hours since leaving Lode Star, hungry, thirsty, and dirty, I swing open the gate and run for the door. I made it. Inside I walk around shouting, "I did it!" I shed my clothes, wet and covered with the earth, and take the longest, dearest shower of my life. When I'm clean and dry I leave a message at home that I'm safe and have lived through it all. I drink some juice and try to eat a piece of fruit but can barely swallow.

My physical hunger has become a herald of my hunger for God. I stand for a long time with a strawberry in my hand, weeping.

Finally I take a blanket and book to the couch and settle down gratefully on the cushions. This is the moment I've been waiting for. This is what I've dreamed about. But my mind sees the words on the page and can't take them in. Instead I see a bird fly past the window, a hawk circling the canyon. A fly buzzes in the room, nearby. Four days ago I would have noticed none of them. Now, I wonder who they are, and if they know I can speak their language. How am I going to fit back into my old world, when the world of trees and rivers and birds tugs at my consciousness too? There is the world I always knew, and yet, there is another world. There is so much more. How will I live in both places?

I cannot believe the feeling in my chest. It aches so deeply with all I see. Something in me has truly changed. I feel it welling up inside of me. I was foolish to think the loneliness I experienced on the quest was hard. It cannot compare with what I am feeling now. Of course if I want to, I can put on my sneakers and go back to the river and get rid of this crushing home-sickness and heartache. I can be there in minutes. But

I know that is not the answer. I can postpone the pain, but I cannot avoid it. Ultimately I have to return to the city and find the way to live in both worlds. Maybe it will take a long time. Maybe my heart will always be a little bit broken. How could I expect to feel the connection I have experienced, and not also know the wrench of leaving. But it also occurs to me that home for me will never again be a structure. I have found home inside of me and all around me. Home in creation. I lie back on the couch and let myself cry out all the feelings, the exhaustion and the love. I quested for vision. I knocked. And the door was opened. It is just as it is promised.

> *You are not enclosed within your bodies,*
> *nor confined to houses or fields.*
> *That which is you dwells above the*
> *mountain and roves with the wind.*

> —Kahlil Gibran, *The Prophet*

The transition back into my "city" life was even harder than I expected. It still is. My wilderness spot stayed inside of me and its reference point is always there. It hurts to go to bed at night and look up at a ceiling. Why did we ever begin to shut out the stars? I have tugs at my heart whenever I lock up my house or my car. I remember living with only trust, and no keys.

Upon returning I rearranged my schedule and my sleeping habits so I could walk outside every morning before beginning the work of the day. The sound of the birds and the smell of the air keeps the homesickness at bay. I see squirrels or chipmunks and know they are so much more than incidental creatures inhabiting a human world. I collect the feathers which I find on my path. My communion with the earth is my conversation with the Creator of all things. The conversation never stops. Nor does the learning.

The obvious suggestion might be, why not find a way to live in the woods? But it's not so easy. There are the other lives in my V-formation, and obedience to where God sends me. One goes into the wilderness to be taught, not to stay. Then the task is to come out and carry the message to those with whom you live. We are interconnected. My experience was as much for all who will hear about it as it was for me. Everything we do affects all others. When we really understand that, we will begin to live differently. Thinking autonomously and separately, we still work at life as if we are islands. The consciousness we need to feel is about our relatedness. My friend Liz describes it as the universal breathing. That's what happened to me. I drew that breath.

I learned in the wilderness that all life is of God. We need to listen to the creation that surrounds us. We are well practiced in seeking wisdom from the study of Scripture, which is of course also alive. "In the beginning was the Word, and the Word was with God, and the Word was God" (Gospel of John). We are also comfortable seeking God in familiar forms of worship. We gather together, two or more, and honor the presence of Spirit in our midst. But too easily we begin imposing our considerable fears onto the Word and the gathering, wanting them to be controlled reflections of ourselves, rather than mighty expressions of God's power. The Word and the gathering must be as expansive as the wilderness if we want to know their truths. Each of us in our own heart must face our nakedness. When we gather only with those of like mind, or we read only the words agreed upon by the particular authorities who make us feel secure, then we will find exactly what we sought, and nothing greater.

There is no such authority and no such safety in the wilderness. There is only God. There is your own name being called and your own response. There is the awareness that human beings are stewards, not owners. We are seekers, not authorities. The only authority in the wilderness is God. God. Not an interpretation of God. Just God. Perhaps that is why truth can be found there with such clarity.

The wilderness taught me that wherever we live, by whatever name we were taught to call the Divine, we all have the hunger. But we have grown afraid of the hunger and afraid of the other names by which God is known. We cling never more tenaciously than to the small path and "religious" vision that is our own — and we require the entire universe to see it that same, exact way. Our human arrogance. Finally, God contained. Except that God is found in abandonment, and not in fear.

When the storm raged during my second night on the quest, all the other creatures immediately became a part of the storm. Save me. True to my human being-ness, I had to first resist what I could not understand or control. I searched for ways to reduce my fear (mattress in the shower stall) and have the storm conform to my management. Only when I learned to become a part of the storm too, replacing fear with trust, did I find what I was searching for.

Human fear is the last vestige of the natural man before he accepts God's grace.

—Randy Becton

Six

THE POWERFUL TEACHINGS I have received continue to inform my mind and heart. The joy and tenderness of the red bird's waiting for me has never left. Nor have red birds. Ever since that experience, they seem to find me. Sometimes when I return to that canyon, so many red birds will surround me, singing, that I cannot walk without tears. Often, as I travel, preparing to lead a retreat or give a talk, a red bird will cross my path. It has happened in the middle of cities, in the country, in the mountains, at the shore. Once the bird was sitting right on the doorstep of a church as I entered to speak. Whenever the red bird appears, that particular gathering is always powerful in some dimension well beyond my understanding.

During the writing of this book the red bird was outside my window or at my feet each day. It was an equal "noncoincidence" that just as I was writing the story about Gabe, the Laity Lodge employee who visited me during the first afternoon of my vision quest, there was a knock on the door at Lode Star, where I was staying. Gabe stood in the door. I had not previously seen him since our encounter in the wilderness, five years before, even though I had been at Laity countless times. It is confirmation to me that beyond the material world of cause and effect, there is a dimension of spirit waiting for our recognition. We see such a small piece of all the wonder surrounding us.

In reading through these pages I have noticed many things: the length of the grief process; the way God must *continue* to be followed and pursued; and the fact that yesterday's understandings of the Divine are already old. It's only the immediate day and the moment right before me that matter. There is so much to learn, and I see the degree to which I've limited years of intake with fear. It is clear that I never saw more than I was willing to risk seeing. I also note how often the same lessons were repeated. I have learned and re-learned and relearned *again* lessons about not "clinging" to what you love. Obviously this is a particularly important teaching for me. I also saw that when I was in the abyss following my family's death, I needed to find within myself the same response which freed me during the night of the wilderness storm: to look into darkness and see light.

Many of the truths presented to me at the Sun Dance, when I was twenty-four years old, were identical to the truths I finally incorporated during my vision quest, almost twenty years later. At twenty-four, I wasn't nearly ready to contain them. Truth has to fall on fertile soil. And in a way, all the intervening circumstances which I experienced during those years were essential parts of my soil's preparation. Our journeys are evolutions.

I recognize the importance of seeing. Perception is what matters most. If my "seeing" does not expand, neither does my faith. Any fear which limits seeing is extremely costly. Seeing is crucial. That's why it is essential to seek vision and create enough silence in one's life to listen to God. We never see more than we are willing to.

I noted the number of times I wept when I first encountered something of importance, even if I understood it very little, or not at all. Nevertheless, something in me was moved. The presence of that "knowing" or intuition gives me great comfort. It says that the sound of what is genuine resonates in each person. This reminds me to pay attention when I am affected by something. Pay attention, and pursue.

Finally, I am aware that most of the freedom, beauty, and joy I have found required risk. I had to be willing to suspend all the conclusions I already had, in order to find the next truths God was revealing. You cannot be safe and also see. You choose.

I think of the words, "No man can serve two masters." They aren't idle words. You can't have life on your own terms and also the Kingdom. It's a matter of knowing what you want more than you want anything. I am learning to listen (pay attention) to everything. Truth surprises me. It does not always come in the way I anticipate it will. I have found it in traditions different from my own and in people with the least bearing or stature. The hardest to admit is that I have often found truth in places (people/traditions) about whom I've had a lot of judgment. God is in everything. That knowledge alone, if grasped, is enough.

Ultimately God remains mystery to me. Sometimes friend, or father, mother, listener, guide, lover, distant ... silent. Always he says, WILL YOU FOLLOW ME? Even if there's nothing to give you stability? Even if you can't understand where I'm leading you? Even if you must wait for the things you desire? Even in the darkness? Will you risk your incarnation to follow the mystery? Will you listen to the earth and let it speak? Will you follow me into the wilderness?

1990–95

Prayer for the Earth

I sit at the foot of a bluff which has slowly been eroded by glacier, wind, and water. I think of the erosion inside of me — the places God is trying to wear smooth. I read a friend's poem, "Offering of Tears," written at the conclusion of a day of fasting. He writes of offering God his tears, and ends by saying, "I have nothing else to offer you."

I think about that. I have bought so many gifts this summer. Wedding gifts, birthday gifts, hostess gifts, thank you gifts. But what do I have to give *you*, God? What would please you that I have?

A flock of gulls flies overhead. They are so beautiful, their black wings against the morning's blue sky. Last night I watched that same sky, covered with stars. I feel the ocean water which laps at my toe. I walk among the rocks, picking up quartz and crystal. What do I have to give *you?*

I close my eyes and listen. You say to me, "Love the beauty of my creation." I wait. There must be more. But there is no more. And I am left hearing the words again. Love the beauty of my creation.

Prayer for the Creatures

To change feels very fearsome to me, God. I like my old consciousness. I hold it close and notice the way it is familiar to my innermost parts. I have no idea what you mean when you call me to extravagant love.

"Come to the well," you say. "Come, follow me."

I press my ear to the living rock of the well, listening to my life. Truth be told, I am afraid to be free. There is so much security in the way I've always thought.

In the way I've always thought about you. In the neat compartment where I keep you.

"Come to the well."

I dip my bucket deep into your unfathomable water. I lower my life into your chambers. Into the arms of you living Presence.

And you take my pain, my fear, my brokenness, my timid, "Yes," and illuminate it with your light.

I come to the well and hear my name.

Prayer for the Heavens

Last night I slept alone under the stars on top of Circle Bluff. Off and on during the night I watched the constellations, noting that they appeared in different locations above my head as the night progressed. Lying still, on my back, it was difficult to keep remembering that the stars were not moving, *I* was. Suddenly that struck me in its fullness.

I was lying on a living globe of seas, rivers, canyons ...lying somewhere in the midst of vast space...and the earth underneath me, and all its oceans, mountains and valleys, was slowly,

> deliberately,
> majestically,
> turning.

The magnificent order of things. The wonder that we are affected by, and affect, the movement of the stars. The knowledge that there is a fire to catch, and it burns in each of us. The knowing that we see a fraction of all that is. And it is good.

The mystery of who we really are is so extraordinary. How can our lives become so full that God calls, and we do not even hear? How can we miss that we are in the presence of extravagant Love?

Prayer for the Winged Ones

I opened the garage door this morning to pull out my trash barrel for the weekly ritual. As I struggled with the lid, a small noise startled me. Almost a musical note, above my head. Looking up, I saw a bluish dove sitting on the top rafter. She had apparently gotten trapped inside. For a moment my eyes held her eyes, and I imagined how frightened she must have been...or *was*.

It was hard to believe that such a winged being — a creature who is able to fly beneath the sun — who knows the intimacy of sunrise — let herself get caught in such a dark place. Slowly I walked back to the outside door, and pushed it open all the way. I let in the sky and whispered to the bird,

"You can go, if you want to. You're free."

She hesitated for a moment, then gracefully spread her wings and dipped lightly from the rafter to the level of the door. Finding the opening, she quickly flew toward the light. In one breath she caught the wind and was gone.

I think the bird was me.

SILENCE

I need not shout my faith. Thrice eloquent
Are quiet trees and the green listening sod;
Hushed are the stars, whose power is never spent;
The hills are mute: yet how they speak of God!

—Charles Hanson Towne